SpringerBriefs on Pioneers in Science and Practice

Volume 32

Series Editor

Hans Günter Brauch, Peace Research and European Security Studies, Mosbach, Baden-Württemberg, Germany

Marek Thee · Nils Petter Gleditsch ·
Stein Tønnesson · Marta Bivand Erdal
Editors

Marek Thee: My Story

A Journey through the 20th Century

Editors
Marek Thee
(1918–1999), Peace Research Institute Oslo
(PRIO)
Oslo, Norway

Stein Tønnesson [ID]
Peace Research Institute Oslo (PRIO)
Oslo, Norway

Nils Petter Gleditsch [ID]
Peace Research Institute Oslo (PRIO)
Oslo, Norway

Norwegian University of Science
and Technology (NTNU)
Trondheim, Norway

Marta Bivand Erdal [ID]
Peace Research Institute Oslo (PRIO)
Oslo, Norway

Acknowledgement:
The cover photograph and other photos in this book are family pictures provided by the daughter of Marek Thee.
Financial support for the editing was provided by the Fritt Ord Foundation, Oslo, Norway.

ISSN 2194-3125   ISSN 2194-3133   (electronic)
SpringerBriefs on Pioneers in Science and Practice
ISBN 978-3-031-16904-5   ISBN 978-3-031-16905-2   (eBook)
https://doi.org/10.1007/978-3-031-16905-2

This Springer imprint is published by the registered company Springer Nature Switzerland AG
The registered company address is: Gewerbestrasse 11, 6330 Cham, Switzerland

Contents

Chapter 1
An International Scholar with a Dramatic Life

Marta Bivand Erdal, Nils Petter Gleditsch, and Stein Tønnesson

Marek Thee lived a dramatic life amidst some of the 20th century's most tragic conflicts. This autobiography was written in the early 1990s. We meet him as a young leftist student in the Free City of Danzig (Gdańsk) before the Nazi takeover; as an advocate of the Jewish Zionist cause in Palestine during and after the Second World War; as a diplomat, foreign service official and scholar in the post-war Polish Republic; as a Polish representative on the Commission for Supervision and Control of the Geneva agreements on Indochina and Laos; as a foreign affairs analyst specializing on Asian affairs in Warsaw of the 1960s; and eventually, for the last 30 years of his life, as a peace researcher at the Peace Research Institute Oslo (PRIO) and the Norwegian Human Rights Institute, once again in exile from his native Poland.

Marek Thee was a fighter with a typewriter. As the bibliography at the end of this volume reveals, he published extensively in Polish and English. Marek always held strong convictions. In the early 1930s, he could travel freely between Danzig and Poland, where he became an ardent opponent of Marshal Józef Piłsudski's regime. It took from him his passport. Paradoxically, this saved his life. While his family moved to Poland in 1938, after the *Kristallnacht*, and later succumbed in the Holocaust, he managed to get on a transport to British Palestine.

Marek Thee spent World War II in Palestine after his dramatic flight to escape Nazism. While there, he engaged in two parallel struggles: one for a Jewish socialist homeland, the other for a free Poland. In his characteristic fighting spirit, Marek Thee engaged in the publication of pamphlets and newsletters in Palestine – for both his favoured causes.

His texts in the *Biuletyn Wolnej Polski*, the *Bulletin of free Poland* show a vast scope of interests. Written first and foremost for Polish language readers in Palestine, they focus on issues related to the new communist Poland, to perspectives on returning to Poland, criticism of the government-in-exile in London, as well as skepticism to the post-war European democracy, particularly in Germany. Since the *Bulletin* was

M. B. Erdal (✉) · N. P. Gleditsch · S. Tønnesson
Peace Research Institute Oslo (PRIO), Oslo, Norway

© The Author(s) 2023
M. Thee et al. (eds.), *Marek Thee: My Story*, SpringerBriefs on Pioneers in Science and Practice 32, https://doi.org/10.1007/978-3-031-16905-2_1

sponsored by the communist Polish authorities, it is difficult in retrospect to be sure to what extent Marek expresses his own opinions and emotions. At times, he glorifies Stalin. In these memoirs he reflects critically on his former views about Stalin and the Stalinist period. By contrast, his appreciation of the Soviet soldiers' contribution and sacrifice in the defeat of Nazi Germany appears genuine.

Marek Thee's contribution to the struggle for a free Poland through the *Bulletin* should, however, not primarily be seen through the prism of its affiliation with the Polish post-war communist authorities. Rather, his work reflects continued faith in and urge to fight for social justice and global peace and at the same time, a deep-seated sentiment for his homeland and its culture and literature. He writes, for instance, with great engagement about the establishment of the UN, in early January 1946, reflecting a strong conviction in the promise of international cooperation, and the absolute need for world peace. While in Israel after 1948 he was also instrumental in the publication of a translation to Hebrew of the Polish national epos *Pan Tadeusz*. References to this epos are visible in his writings on political affairs, directly and indirectly. In one case he quotes a famous passage from *Pan Tadeusz* on the experiences of Polish youth fighting for Napoleon in his Russia campaign in 1812.[1] The names of people with whom he worked in producing the *Bulletin*, and others whom he later in his consular role assisted in their return to Poland, such as Brandstaetter, Broniewski, Lec and Stern, were all well-known Polish language poets.

After the defeat of Nazi Germany, Marek Thee obtained a new Polish passport from the Polish Republic (renamed People's Republic in 1952) and became a Polish consular representative to the state of Israel after its establishment in 1948.

In 1952, he was recalled to Poland, where, shortly after, he was transferred to the Polish Institute of Foreign Affairs. As he recounts in these memoirs, this was directly due to his Jewish background and events preceding Stalin's death. He spent the next three years studying, picking up ambitions to pursue higher education which had earlier been curtailed by the war. He first took a master's degree and then a doctorate in history, with focus on the Middle East.

In 1955, Marek Thee joined the International Commission for Supervision and Control for the 1954 Geneva agreement on Indochina, serving first in Saigon and then in Laos. By the time he joined, the Commission, which included representatives of India, Canada and Poland, had carried out its most urgent tasks in monitoring the withdrawal of French troops to south of the 17th parallel, and of troops serving the Democratic Republic of Vietnam to north of that line. The political and military partition between North and South Vietnam was meant to last until general elections could be held in the whole country in 1956. As head of the International Commission's Saigon office in 1955, Marek established a close friendship with one of the top Vietnamese communist leaders, the later prime minister Pham Hung. He hailed from the south and served in 1955 as head of North Vietnam's liaison mission in Saigon. Already then, Marek learned to see all of Indochina as an integrated political and military arena. So, in 1956–57, when he was posted to Vientiane as a representative on the Control Commission for Laos, he realized the importance of close cooperation

---

[1] See Thee (1946) Reakcja … under Articles in the bibliography.

between the Vietnamese communist leaders in Hanoi and their Lao allies in the Pathet Lao. Laos could not in Marek's view be treated as a totally separate country. Its politics and civil war had to be understood in an Indochinese context, where neutrality and peace in Laos would depend on neutrality and peace in South Vietnam. Marek thus opposed and prevented attempts by other members of the Control Commission to inspect the border areas to Vietnam and demand the withdrawal of North Vietnamese troops from those areas. The border provinces were controlled by Prince Souphan-nouvong's Pathet Lao movement, which received support, guidance and military training from North Vietnam. To keep control of the border areas was strategically important for Hanoi in case it should decide to resort to renewed armed fighting in South Vietnam to unify the nation. In 1957, after the repressive regime of Ngo Dinh Diem had failed to comply with the agreement reached in Geneva to hold general elections in both parts of Vietnam before July 1956, some south-based communists dug up again the arms they had hidden in 1954. Two years later, the Party leaders in Hanoi decided to support a growing insurgency in the South and build what would be known as the Ho Chi Minh trail through Laos to supply fighters, arms and other provisions.

At that time, Hanoi's decision did not conform to advice from either Beijing or Moscow. At a meeting between China's leader Mao Zedong and Soviet leader Nikita Khrushchev on 2 October 1959, they agreed that there should be no repetition of the mistake made by Josef Stalin when he authorized Kim Il Sung to invade South Korea in 1950. They did not want a repeat in Laos or Vietnam. Khrushchev imagined that an escalation of the conflict in Laos would provoke a US intervention that would crush the Democratic Republic of (North) Vietnam.[2]

Marek Thee stood by Hanoi. A procedure had been established for the Polish representatives on the International Control Commissions for Vietnam, Cambodia and Laos to receive their instructions from Hanoi rather than from Moscow or their own government in Warsaw. Marek was not the only Polish representative to be seen as representing the interests of North Vietnam. Yet, in Indochinese diplomatic circles, he became known as a quintessential hardliner, going much further than China, the USSR and his own Polish government in his dedicated support for North Vietnam and the Pathet Lao.[3] With the Sino-Soviet split in 1960, Mao's China changed opinion and came out in full support of Hanoi's war for South Vietnam, while the Soviet Union remained skeptical.

In 1961, when negotiations began between the US, USSR and other countries for what would become the 23 July 1962 International Agreement on the Neutrality of Laos, the International Control Commission for the 1954 Geneva Convention was

---

[2] Memorandum of Conversation of NS Khrushchev with Mao Zedong, Beijing, 2 October 1959. English translation as document No. 3 in *Cold War International History Bulletin*, No. 12–13, Fall/Winter 2001, p. 1270.

[3] Mieczyslaw Maneli (1971) *War of the Vanquished*. New York: Harper and Row: 116, 182–185, Laurent Cesari (2007) *Les grandes puissances et le Laos, 1954–1964*. Arras: Artois Presses Université, 39. Arthur J Dommen (2001) *The Indochinese Experience of the French and the Americans: Nationalism and Communism in Cambodia, Laos, and Vietnam*. Bloomington. IN: Indiana University Press, 311–312.

revived after having been dormant since July 1958.[4] In April 1961, Marek Thee therefore returned on a second mission to Laos. The 1962 agreement guaranteed the sovereignty and neutrality of the deeply divided Lao state. From the perspective of US President John F. Kennedy, the agreement was both a means to end the civil war in Laos and to prevent the flow of provisions from North to South Vietnam through Lao territory. The insurgency in South Vietnam had taken off for real with the founding of the National Liberation Front for South Vietnam (NLF) in December 1960. Marek's sympathy for Hanoi's cause now brought him into trouble with Moscow as well as Warsaw. Moscow was consumed by its wish to obtain a Western withdrawal from Berlin and was prepared to make concessions to the US in the distant Vietnam and Laos. Poland wanted to purchase American grain. Hence Moscow and Warsaw were both keen to respect the new Geneva agreement. Hanoi and Marek Thee were not.

Marek's autobiography in this volume as well as his 1973 book *Notes of a Witness* recount his decision to work with Hanoi and Pathet Lao rather than seek instructions from Warsaw or Moscow. He relates the criticism he received from the Polish and Soviet governments. The latter, in his view, was always ready to trade away the interests of the Indochinese peoples against Western concessions in Europe. On a return trip to Warsaw in Spring 1963, Marek was told that he was naïve and idealistic. Nevertheless, he was reconfirmed as a member of the Polish delegation and once again returned to Laos.

This time his stay did not last long. On 23 September 1963, Prince Souvanna Phouma, the neutralist prime minister of Laos, met President John F. Kennedy in the White House. The Prince said 'he felt, in fact he was convinced, the Soviet Ambassador was doing what he could to help ensure observance of the Geneva Agreements, but he did not seem to have direct influence on the Polish Commissioner of the International Control Commission.' Prince Souvanna told Kennedy that 'Marek Thee, the Polish Commissioner, always sided with the PL' (Pathet Lao). So, when Kennedy suggested it might be helpful to have a change in the Polish Commissioner, Prince Souvanna thought 'this was a good idea' and promised to take it up with Nikita Khrushchev during a visit to Moscow on his way back to Vientiane.[5]

Four months later, in January 1964, Marek Thee was back as a foreign policy researcher in Warsaw. His Indochinese adventure was over. By then, both South Vietnam's president Ngo Dinh Diem and US president John F Kennedy had been murdered, and Khrushchev's days as Soviet leader were counted. Indochina now entered the escalatory phase of what came to be known as the Vietnam War, now also with heavy support from the Soviet Union and its allies in the Warsaw Pact.

After returning from Indochina to Warsaw, Marek worked as an analyst and researcher for the Polish Institute of Foreign Affairs, directly under the Ministry of Foreign Affairs. It is worth underscoring that it was the Central Committee of

---

[4] Cesari, *op.cit.,* p. 79.

[5] Kennedy Library, National Security Files, Countries Series, Laos: General, 10/63–11/63. Confidential. Drafted by Toumayan. Published in the *Foreign Relations of the United States (FRUS)* series as doc. 489, Memorandum of Conversation, Washington, September 23, 1963, 5–6 p.m. Meeting between the President and the Prime Minister of Laos.

the Polish Communist Party that controlled public events, institutions and publications. Marek Thee found it more and more difficult to toe the party line, as his own retrospective reflections reveal. Due to his diplomatic engagements, his scholarly publications had to appear under the pseudonym Marek Gdański.

In 1968, he became a victim of a new wave of Polish anti-Semitism and lost his job. Władysław Gomułka, the chairman of the Polish United Workers' Party, gave a speech saying that we want Poland to be for the Poles and that Zionists should leave. This was followed by a nation-wide campaign to force people of Jewish origin out of Poland. Marek Thee and his family were among those. Most of the Jews still living in Poland at the time, who had survived the Holocaust or returned after the war, were forced – or encouraged – to emigrate, the assumption being they would go to Israel. Current estimates suggest that between 13,000 and 20,000 people left Poland as a result. Jews from Poland were scattered around the world, including Scandinavia, although only a handful of people ended up in Norway. Surprisingly perhaps, Marek Thee did not choose to go back to Israel, where he had already lived. Johan Galtung offered him a position at PRIO, which he accepted. His wife Erna was from Vienna – they had met in Palestine, and their two daughters Maya and Halina had grown up in Poland. All were now uprooted and taken to a foreign country in the north.

During his time at PRIO, Marek dedicated himself to an international struggle against the arms race and particularly against military research and development which he held responsible for driving the Cold War arms dynamics. He fought vigilantly for disarmament, arms control, peace and development. He championed the idea of establishing a global disarmament fund for development. His major project at PRIO, for which he had been hired, was to edit a new journal, the *Bulletin of Peace Proposals*. Its goal was 'to present systematically, to compare and discuss in the light of general peace research theory various plans, proposals and ideas for development, justice and peace.' The journal adopted 'a broad definition of the term "peace proposals"' (Thee 1970: 3). Each issue was divided into two sections, a documentation section with summaries of the proposals, and an analytical section with discussion of a set of proposals on a specific topic. Although the project was originally conceived by Galtung, it suited Marek's temperament well. He took it to heart and put his personal stamp on the journal, first in two trial issues and then as a quarterly journal from 1970.

From the start, *BPP* had an Advisory Council with distinguished academics from the Nordic countries, as well as an Editorial Committee, mainly with colleagues from PRIO. Nevertheless, there was little question that this was Marek's journal, where he defined the relevant topics and made the editorial decisions. It was his choice to shift the journal in the direction of more analysis and fewer proposals. The first published issue contained abstracts of 54 peace proposals and six short articles. In later issues, the articles became longer and more numerous. Since 1989, following Marek's retirement from PRIO, the journal was taken over by a new editor. Since mid-1992 it has been published under a new name, *Security Dialogue*, eventually adopting a critical security studies profile.

From his arrival in Oslo in 1968 until his retirement in 1988, Marek Thee was Nils Petter Gleditsch's colleague at PRIO. In 1980–82, he served as PRIO supervisor for Stein Tønnesson's dissertation on the outbreak of war in Indochina and, in 1988, welcomed Tønnesson back to PRIO with a doctoral project on the Vietnamese revolution. Marek urged Stein to travel to Vietnam and interview his old acquaintances. PRIO Researcher Marta Bivand Erdal never met Marek. She came to PRIO in 2007, eight years after her compatriot had passed away. Yet, with her Polish background, she was fascinated by his life story and got in touch with his daughters. In an interview with Marek's youngest daughter, Halina, Marta became aware of Marek's unpublished memoirs. She wrote a blog post on Marek Thee in 2019 published in the series PRIO Stories, now a chapter in Stein Tønnesson, ed. *Lives in Peace Research: the Oslo Stories* (Springer, 2022), and helped compile the bibliography of Marek's Polish writings in this volume.

We are impressed by Marek's qualities as an energetic, hard-working, independent-minded and dedicated scholar. While *BPP* was his main project at PRIO, he also lectured extensively, participated in numerous conferences, and engaged in a number of research projects. Much of this activity was channeled back into articles and special issues of *BPP*. Marek also participated actively in the decision-making at the Institute, which for most of his time at PRIO was based on a collective management style. He served as Director of the institute for two years (1981–83).

His treatment by the Polish authorities did not make him an embittered anti-Communist. While his commitment to democracy in Poland and other countries in the then Soviet sphere of interest comes out clearly in his writings, he portrayed the Cold War with its galloping arms race as basically a serious failure of the international system. He went to conferences in Moscow and to meetings organized by the Soviet-sponsored International Institute for Peace (IIP). Indeed, his somewhat acrimonious departure from PRIO occurred after the then Director of PRIO felt that he had overstepped his mark in agreeing to represent IIP at a meeting at the UN. Marek had hoped to continue to do research in an emeritus position after reaching the mandatory Norwegian retirement age at 70. In public, he loyally passed the editorship of *BPP* to his successor (Thee 1988), but in private he was strongly disappointed that PRIO's leadership would not allow him to continue working at the institute.

In the event, his separation from PRIO did not prove as destructive as it might have. Marek was invited to join the Norwegian Human Rights Institute, directed by his old PRIO colleague, Asbjørn Eide, and worked there until his death in 1999. He integrated well in his new academic home and remained active until the end.

Marek Thee's autobiography was probably written soon after the death of his wife Erna in 1989. We do not know why he did not publish it before his own death. After his death, the manuscript remained in the custody of his daughters. When Marta Bivand Erdal contacted them in preparation for the portrait she wrote of Marek Thee, we realized the importance of making it publicly available. It gives a vivid description of a dramatic life, an introduction to main themes in 20th century world history and a testimony to the worth of engaged peace research.

Marek Thee's manuscript has been subjected to some light technical editing by Gee Berry, Nils Petter Gleditsch, Halina Thee, and Stein Tønnesson. Following

Marek's own preference, it has been edited to fit the style of British English. The spelling of names and titles in Norwegian, French, Vietnamese and Laotian has been checked by the editors. Any errors remain our responsibility.

The format follows Marek's own, with some inconsistencies corrected. Thus, there are several deviations from the PRIO style as well as the house style for this book series.

The original manuscript as received from Halina Thee has been archived at the National Archives of Norway (Riksarkivet) as part of PRIO's historical archive (Privatarkiv 1955, archive code Fy).

We acknowledge generous help in preparing Marek Thee's memoirs for publication from Halina Thee, and also valuable assistance from Gee Berry, Halvor Berggrav, Hans Günter Brauch, Selma Kheloufi Hansen, Younes Kheloufi Hansen, Daniel Kjelling, Agnete Schjønsby, and Indigo Trigg-Hauger. Finally, we express our gratitude to the Fritt Ord foundation for its financial support.

Oslo, 9 March 2022

References

Thee, Marek (1970) Prefatory Note. *Bulletin of Peace Proposals* 1(1): 3–4. [Signed: The Editor]
Thee, Marek (1988) Letter from the Editor. *Bulletin of Peace Proposals* 19(3/4): 243.

Chapter 2
My Story. A Journey Through the 20th Century

Marek Thee

2.1 At the End of the Itinerary

On September 11, 1989, my beloved wife Erna suddenly passed away. Cancer. How can I describe the shock? All at once, unexpected, I lost a dear and faithful lifelong companion. With Erna I had shared joy and sorrow for almost 50 years, since we met as refugees in Palestine back in 1940, she coming from Nazi Austria and I from Nazi Danzig. We had proceeded harmoniously through a stormy life in Palestine and Israel, then in Poland, in Indochina, and again in Poland, before finally, in 1968, finding refuge and a new life in Norway.

In the aftermath of September 1989, trauma channelled into reflection. I felt as if I had come to the end of my itinerary in this life. What had it been like?

The passing away of Erna coincided with another agonizing moment in my life. I was on the verge of moving from a highly active academic professional life, as a peace researcher in contemporary international relations, to retirement. This took place in a mood of disillusionment with institutional peace research. I was perturbed by the ongoing shift from what I saw as an independent value-loaded scholarly discipline aimed at transcending violence in international and human affairs towards an Establishment-oriented acceptance of power relations in world politics as an almost immutable reality. Preoccupied with the centrality of military hardware and its employment, a sizeable part of established peace research had slid into strategic studies.

In a paper presented in November 1988 at a UNESCO meeting of experts in Lima, on "Trends and Evaluation of Peace and Conflict Research in Social and Human Sciences", I intimated my disenchantment with what seemed to be a drift

Marek Thee: Deceased

M. Thee (✉)
Peace Research Institute Oslo (PRIO), Oslo, Norway

© The Author(s) 2023
M. Thee et al. (eds.), *Marek Thee: My Story*, SpringerBriefs on Pioneers in Science and Practice 32, https://doi.org/10.1007/978-3-031-16905-2_2

into opportunism in the scholarly discipline to which I had been attached for over 20 years. I noted:

Historically, peace research can be seen as the heir in the domain of social sciences of the age-old longings for the 'utopia' of a just and peaceful society – for brotherhood, freedom and equitable human relations, nationally and internationally, as expressed in the philosophies of various social and religious thinkers, and in recent centuries, in the aspirations of the American, French, Russian, Mexican and anti-colonial revolutions. If there is a basic lesson to be learned from this experience, it is that change through the use of violence does not fully free society. Even after revolution, violence tends to permeate the body politics. Only non-violent change seems to have a potential for lasting peaceful transformation of human relations.

And further:

In distinction to peace research, strategic studies do not disapprove of military power as a dominant factor in international relations. They follow the 'realistic' paradigm, which perceives military power and organized violence as governing the relations between nations. No attempt is made to challenge this state of affairs. Essentially, strategic studies adhere – explicitly or implicitly – to a *status quo* orientation, pursuing in fact ways and means to stabilize and petrify the world military order … Ethics, moral constraints and human security as against military security – these are secondary to the endeavours of strategic studies … Thus, we note a clear clash between the vision and models of the worlds aspired by peace research on the one hand and by strategic studies on the other hand.[i]

Such dilemmas have not been unique to peace research. For one thing, they are common in international relations studies, where the 'realist' school is predominant. International relations today are essentially power relations. I was nevertheless troubled that also peace research – the last scholarly station in my life – was moving to assimilate this 'reality' as a seemingly eternal wisdom. Was there no alternative? Is violence an innate feature of international and human relations? The internationalist human dream which served as an inspiration for many generations in modern times – is it only a delusion?

My nonconformist position on the substance of peace research was to sour my retirement. Coming together with my refusal to submit to a newly introduced semi-authoritarian order in my mother institution, the International Peace Research Institute, Oslo (PRIO), it resulted in a situation where the new Director refused to grant me working space to continue my research after retirement. Happily, I was offered alternative working space and facilities at the Norwegian Institute of Human Rights.[1]

In the meantime, the world scene, the subject of my studies, had moved into a state of agitation. A profound transformation was in the making. The Cold War, which had permeated international relations since World War II, was beginning to fade away. Stalinist authoritarian bureaucracies in Central Eastern Europe crumbled under the onslaught of the people, in domino-like fashion. And the Berlin Wall, the symbol of a divided world, was suddenly toppled.

---

[1] Now the Norwegian Centre for Human Rights (NCHS) at the University of Oslo. (The editors.)

There was both hope and anxiety in the air. In a paper on the 'velvet' revolutions in Central Eastern Europe, I pointed to the "lights and shades of systemic transformation":

The beginnings were full of light and hope. Fundamental political changes had taken place. The new configuration is, however, still in the making. National symbols and rituals as well as religious fundamentalist-like fervour and socio-political vision clash and interact to occupy the void left after the abolition of totalitarian regimes. Hatred of communism, intertwined with the influence of the Church, tends to favour conservative values ... After the abhorrent long-standing deprivations under the communist regime, the pendulum seems to be oscillating to the right ... We should not underestimate the explosive nature of the mix of high economic predicaments and the revival of extreme nationalistic fundamentalism.[ii]

These trends were not encouraging. I was worried by the rise in doctrinaire nationalism and religious obduracy in combination with a dearth of truly equitable socio-economic reform programmes as alternatives to both the Stalinist-type exploitative command economy and to greedy capitalism, to parallel the democratic human rights essentials. It was difficult to retain unshaded optimism.

I felt a compulsion to look back on my life experience, my accomplishments and failures. To sum them up. How had I spent my years? How had I confronted the good and the evil? Were my ups and downs fully part of my individual making or were they also part of the upheavals and annals of the 20th century? How, then, did I meet the challenges of this century? How much of my life trajectory was well contrived and how much was it simply chance, moulded and carried by the tide of events? Are there lessons to learn, even if my retrospection may be subjective?

For one thing, there is something unusual and unique in my life history and career. I have lived in many worlds and been witness to major developments in some key corners of the globe, East and West, North and South. My experience as political activist, diplomat, historian and researcher in contemporary international relations has covered a broad span – from the interwar period until the decline of the Cold War and the pursuit of a militarized "new world order" following the Gulf War. I have observed at close range the rise of fascism and the Nazi takeover in Danzig (Gdańsk). I have lived through the ascent and fall of communism, with long years under the rule of "real socialism", a 'socialism' imposed by the Leninist-Stalinist rule. I have known the bitter sensation of being a refugee, both in the pre- and post-war periods. I have intimately felt the tragedy of the Holocaust, with the loss of my whole family. I have been witness to the birth of Israel. I have then been employed in the Polish diplomatic service in Israel, Vietnam and Laos, not as a career officer but through the working of the wheel of chance. And, culminating my professional life, I have developed a scholarly career as a peace researcher in international affairs. Somehow, all my life history has been intertwined with the course of history and human fate in the 20th century. A political animal in a turbulent world.

2.2   Pre-war Poland, Nazi Danzig and the Flight to Palestine

Again and again my tangled life story came before my eyes. Born in Rzeszów, in southern Poland, days after the guns of World War I fell silent, a child of a Jewish 'shtetl', I landed with my family at the close of the 1920s in the Free City of Danzig (now Gdańsk), a post-Versailles enclave in northern Poland contested by the Germans and the Poles. My primary education in my hometown of Rzeszów, and my secondary education in Gdańsk and Gdynia, across the Polish-Danzig border, was in Polish schools. Polish history and culture permeated my thought and senses.

What sticks in my mind from my youth in the interwar years is an atmosphere of nationalist intolerance and discrimination: antisemitism in Poland and the onslaught of the Nazis in Germany and Danzig. This was part of my daily agony on the street and at school, coinciding with a hard morning-to-evening toiling for subsistence at home. My family was of a lower merchant middle class which had to work hard for a livelihood. The range of ideas at home was almost limited to prayers for being better off.

Out of these predicaments grew my life dream of a world free of hatred, national prejudice and exploitation. The yearning for human brotherhood, social justice and international understanding would stay with me for my whole life. The two poles of early attraction, as a kind of anchorage and as symbols of emancipation, became on the one hand a homeland in a socialist Palestine, and on the other hand socialist internationalist transformation, as hoped for with the revolutionary change in the Soviet state. As a youngster in Rzeszów, I joined the left-Zionist youth movement *Shomer Hatzair* (The Young Guard), and in Danzig I found my way to the communist youth organization.

As in most contemporary student movements, in these early affiliations there was little of well-considered, learned choices. They reflected rather an emotional, value-loaded quest for a way out from the hopelessness and quandary of a social and national nature. My initial introduction to Marxism reinforced this mental frame. In line with these sensibilities was an eagerness for action – to participate actively in the battles for revolutionary change.

Without fully realizing the dangers involved, or perhaps even tempting fate and visualizing heroic valour, I was soon to became entangled in a triple clandestine activity. On the one hand, on instructions from the communist underground, I lent a hand to the furtive distribution of anti-Nazi leaflets in workers' suburbs. On the other hand, I engaged in veiled socialist propaganda at school, disseminating Marxist literature and trying to win my fellow pupils over to the ideas of socialism. At the same time, I served as a courier between the underground communist organizations in Danzig and Gdynia, carrying – in school uniform – party materials across the Polish-Danzig border. There was elation and nervousness in these undertakings. A special aspect was the necessity of hiding my political activity from my parents, who violently disapproved of my convictions.

Matters came to a head on the eve of World War II. In 1938, immediately after graduating from the secondary school in Gdynia, I was deprived of my Polish citizenship. No reason was offered, but it was obvious that this was a penalty for my left-wing leanings. The eye of the Polish security authorities was ubiquitous. The peculiar thing was that I was the only one in my family to fall victim to this discriminatory measure. My parents, two sisters and a brother retained Polish citizenship and managed, following the November 1938 *Kristallnacht* pogrom, to flee to Poland ... only to fall prey to the Holocaust. I found myself all alone, bottled up in Nazi Danzig, with a Nazi stateless passport, the *Danziger Staatenlosen Pass*, in my pocket. It was a desperate situation. No country to flee to.

The only hope seemed to be Palestine. Though the British colonial administration in Palestine had closed the doors to Jewish immigration, illegal refugee transports did manage from time to time to pierce the blockade. It was such an illegal transport that I succeeded in joining. This was an odd operation, mounted by an arrangement between the Nazi authorities and the Jewish community in Danzig. The Nazis seized the entire property of the Jewish community, including even the cemetery; then, as a kind of *Endlösung*, to make Danzig *Judenrein*, they let the remaining members of the Jewish community leave Danzig[2]. The first transport of approximately 500 Jews, myself included, departed from Danzig in the direction of the Black Sea in the beginning of March 1939. Only a few personal belongings could be taken along.

The transport proceeded in sealed carriages, with curtained windows, under Gestapo supervision, through Germany and Austria to the Hungarian border. There, it was taken over by a Jewish organization linked to the Zionist underground in Palestine. We reached the Romanian port of Galati, where we were joined by about 200 young Romanian and Bulgarian Jews. Under the cover of night, we then boarded an old Greek cargo vessel 'Astir', which was primitively furnished under deck with three layers of makeshift wooden galleries, to accommodate, not without difficulty, our sizeable party.

We were told that we would reach Palestine and land illegally in about a week. Instead, our odyssey through the Black Sea, the Dardanelles and around the Eastern Mediterranean was to last nearly four months! We left Danzig on March 3, 1939 and landed in Palestine exhausted on June 28 that year. This was a gruesome journey. We were all the time kept under deck so as not to be visible. Conditions became appalling and extremely unsanitary. We had little food and very scarce drinking water. At Easter, as we approached the shores of Palestine, we were intercepted by the British. We were brought to the port of Haifa and, with a load of some food and fresh water, sent back to Greece. But we tried again. Before the anticipated second landing, at night, we shifted from the 'Astir' to a large fishing boat, packed in like sardines, and set course for the shore. Then the motor broke down and we were once more intercepted. But this time we were finally admitted to Palestine: we were included into the quota of the May 1939 White Paper, which opened the gates of the country to a limited number of refugees. My *Danziger Staatenlosen Pass* remained

---

[2] www.jewishgen.org/yizkor/danzig/dan267.html (H.T.)

on the bottom of the Mediterranean. In order to hide our identities, we had been ordered to throw overboard all personal documents.

And yet, identity is not a piece of paper. There exists such a thing as human identity and historical memory. Such experiences tend to nerve these sensibilities. They leave a sore trace in the human soul which calls for the redemption of the benevolent and righteous in human beings.

2.3   Three Worlds in the Promised and Disputed Land

As fate would have it, I was to stay in Palestine and then in Israel for 13 years. This was a portentous period in my life. It catapulted me into a career I had never thought of when I disembarked in Palestine. My inner strivings for a dignified life in freedom, in a radically changed, more just world, led me first to engage in Jewish-Palestinian issues intertwined with World War II concerns, then to initiate a "Free Poland" movement, to finally be drawn into the Polish consular-diplomatic service.

I arrived in Palestine only weeks before the outbreak of World War II. In the first days of September 1939, following the invasion of Poland by Nazi Germany, I volunteered to military service. However, the British authorities, fearing Arab-Jewish disequilibrium in the war effort, were then not willing to incorporate Jewish units into their army.

This was a time of gloom. The Ribbentrop-Molotov Pact and the start of the war in Europe made the world look bleak. No word came through from my family in Poland. And in Palestine, the Arab-Jewish conflict lingered on, while the plight of Jewish refugees fleeing Europe pressed for a fair and equitable solution.

Dismayed, I looked for an opportunity for political engagement. Before long, I was contacted by an underground group of young Jewish intellectuals who had split away from the Communist Party of Palestine (CPP) to establish a separate organization under the name of *Emet* (The Truth). The background for this split lay in *Emet*'s repudiation of Stalinist Comintern policy, which refused to recognize the independent nationhood of the Jewish people because of its dispersion around the world. Subordinated to the Comintern, the CPP adopted an extreme anti-Zionist line that called for a halt to Jewish immigration; it instead pursued the establishment of an Arab Palestine with the denial of the national aspirations of the Jewish population. Organizationally, the Comintern imposed on the CPP a line of 'arabization' which stipulated Arab leadership – even though the majority of members were Jews. The anti-Zionist line of the CPP went so far as to support the anti-Jewish terror during the 1936–39 Arab nationalist insurrection. In international affairs, the CPP approved the 1939 Ribbentrop-Molotov Pact, shifting its position only after Germany's invasion of the Soviet Union in 1941.

In opposition to the CPP, the *Emet* group was striving for the cognizance of the national and cultural rights of the Jewish inhabitants of Palestine (the Yishuv), aiming at Arab-Jewish understanding and cooperation. The nearest to the solution envisaged by *Emet*, and which I cherished, was an Arab-Jewish binational state in

Palestine. This was the line pursued by the *Ihud* (Union) Association, formed in 1942 by the President of the Hebrew University, Dr. Judah Magnes, and the well-known philosopher, Prof. Martin Buber.

Alas, this was not to materialize. The course of World War II, the Jewish Holocaust and the influx of Jewish refugees from Europe as well as from Arab countries on the one hand, and the intransigence of the Palestinian leadership on the other hand, all shifted the cadre of the conflict. Nationalism took over. The establishment of the state of Israel was not accompanied by the founding of an Arab Palestinian state, as envisaged by the UN partition plan of November 1947. The rejection of this plan by the Palestinian leadership and the Arab countries led to a chain of Arab-Israeli wars, with Israel gaining in strength and the position of the Palestinians deteriorating. Instead of a solution, there was escalation of the contest. National incompatibilities seemed to prevail over a policy of sane accommodation.

In 1940, I plunged into the clandestine activity of the *Emet* group. I took over its publication department and became head of the illegal printing office. Students at the Hebrew University introduced me into the Hebrew language and the art of type-setting. In no time, we enlarged our activity to edit not only material concerning internal Palestine problems but also leaflets addressed to the Allied forces who were then camped in large numbers in Palestine and the Middle East. Our appeals to the English-speaking soldiers called for the intensification of the war effort and the opening of a Second Front in Europe. Also, leftist circles in the Greek units turned to us for technical help. We printed materials for them in Greek, in their own wording, aimed at the Greek armed forces in the Middle East.

It was at that time, in illegal activity, that I met Erna. We shared love and common longing for a better world in peace. In Vienna, Erna had belonged to the left-Zionist *Shomer Hatzair*. We were bound by ties of fate: I had lost my whole family; Erna had lost her parents and a younger brother in the Holocaust. We lived until 1947 in Tel-Aviv in a small room on a roof. Erna worked in a textile factory. I was professionally busy in politics, in between earning a living in a brush carpenters' shop. In May 1946, our first daughter, Maya, was born.

One episode then, though grim at the time, served to throw a bridge from the underground activity in the early 1940s to later half-legal and finally legal activity in the "Free Poland" movement. In 1942, while busy with my co-workers in the clandestine printing studio, producing a leaflet to be spread to British and Allied forces, we were surprised by a British police intelligence unit and arrested. This was a dangerous moment: the policemen had orders to shoot if resisted. To pursue political activity aimed at members of the armed forces in active service was, of course, a severe offence, particularly in time of war. However, as we were not trying to subvert the war effort, the court treated us with leniency. After three weeks in the Jaffa prison, we were given suspended six-month sentences. Freed from the prison, we naturally reverted, in more conspiratorial conditions, to our publication activity.

Subsequently, when I moved to work with Polish affairs, the above incident proved of value in my new engagement. Arrested again in spring 1944, while distributing leaflets to Polish officers, I was brought before a police commissioner who already knew my case. After only a night in a police ward, I was released with a warning that whatever I might intend to publish I would have to submit beforehand to censorship. I could not have asked for better terms – almost overnight my activity acquired semi-legal status!

As from 1943, I shifted my field of activity to Polish concerns. My primary impulse to address Polish soldiers came with the appearance on the streets of Tel-Aviv of hundreds of Polish officers from the army of General Anders, recently arrived from the Soviet Union. Through an agreement between Stalin and General Sikorski's Polish government-in-exile, some 75,000 Polish soldiers were allowed to leave the Soviet Union to join Allied armies in the Middle East. They subsequently remained in Palestine and the Middle East as reserve forces, for the eventuality of entering Poland from the West.

I was disturbed meeting these idle Polish officers. This was a conservative legion with leanings to the right-wing, semi-fascist pre-war regime in Poland. My hopes were for a different, socialist and democratic Poland. The fate of Poland, the country of my ancestors, and where I was born, was not indifferent to me. Progressive change in Poland, I felt, portended also a new positive turn in the history of Europe. In my view, rather than merely camping in inactivity in Palestine, the Polish army, as also other Allied soldiers, should move to the most vital battlefields in Europe, to open a Second Front behind the Nazi forces.

Out of these considerations, in a flush of political drive, I started an action which was to lead to the establishment of a Free Poland movement in Palestine and the Middle East, parallel to similar organizations in the Soviet Union and some Western countries. In September 1943, I drafted, duplicated and distributed my first appeal to Polish soldiers. This was an entirely individual initiative. No political body was behind it. My fellow co-workers and friends were only to a small degree interested in Polish affairs; moreover, the communist movement in Palestine was at that time split in many factions, all hotly involved in their own internal problems.

My experience in the editing, printing and publishing of political literature acquired during the *Emet* period now came to good use. I knew the technicalities of printing under clandestine conditions and had access to a Gestetner duplicating machine. Later, I was also able to establish working contacts with legal printing houses.

It took me a few days of intense thought to draft the text of the first leaflet. I opened it with the traditional motto from Polish participation in freedom struggles in many corners of the world: "For Your and Our Freedom, For the Freedom of All Nations". The appeal then urged the soldiers to demand to be transferred to the battlegrounds of Europe – "now – immediately". I signed the leaflet in such a way as to suggest a collective underground endeavour: "Poles–Patriots–Antifascists". After typing the text on an old Polish typewriter, I ran the leaflet off in 300 copies and went to distribute it myself to the Polish officers strolling along Allenby Street, the main thoroughfare in Tel-Aviv.

The effect surpassed all my expectations. The leaflet electrified both the Polish refugee community and members of the Polish army. On the one hand, the Polish military authorities increased their repression of officers and soldiers suspected of leftist progressive views. Some of them were arrested and imprisoned in the mini-concentration camp in Latrun administered by the Polish army. On the other hand, I also received many offers of cooperation.

Encouraged by the resonance, I produced and distributed a second leaflet to Polish soldiers in October 1943. This was formulated in more concrete terms, calling for a return in arms to Poland. It pointed to the example of the Polish units that had been fighting alongside the Soviet army and advancing to the eastern borders of Poland.

The signature on these two leaflets was soon transformed into organizational flesh. In February 1944, a Free Poland movement under the name of "Association of Polish Patriots in the Middle East" was founded in Jerusalem. Soon also, in March 1944, we started to publish a journal: *Bulletin of Free Poland*. It appeared first as a duplicated monthly; then, as from May 1944, as a printed biweekly; and as from January 1945 as a weekly. All in all, during the three years of its existence, until May 1947, we published 141 issues of the journal. Circulation rose from 400 copies at the start to 2500 only a few months later. We concentrated on news from Poland and the course of liberation in Europe. I was in charge of international problems. A large part of the journal was devoted to cultural life and intellectual renewal in liberated Poland, with emphasis on Jewish affairs. I still have a complete set of the journal. Other sets are in the archives in Poland and the Hebrew University in Jerusalem.

We were lucky from the beginning to win the cooperation of prominent journalists and literary men as well as respected high-ranking Army officers who realized that the fate of Poland was inevitably linked to socialist democratic transformation – not least, as determined by the rising role of the Soviet Union in Central Eastern Europe. Among the men of letters were such well-known poets as Władysław Broniewski, Roman Brandstaetter and Anatol Stern. They published in our journal; Broniewski even served as proof-reader of the journal for a while.

Initially we encountered enormous financial difficulties, as sales revenues hardly covered the expenses. We had at times to rely on support from left-Zionist circles. We worked also under great political stress. Most of our collaborators, especially those from the Army, had to stay in hiding. Throughout this initial period, I served as publisher of the journal, my post-office box being the address of the journal. My conspiratorial pseudonym, bestowed on me by my collaborators, was *Płomienny* (The Fiery One).

A turning point came when contact was established with the Free Poland movement in the Soviet Union and, later, with the newly formed authorities in Poland. As the only openly acting representative of our organization in Palestine, I was the first to receive a message offering cooperation. On October 11, 1944, I received a cable from Moscow signed by the later Foreign Minister of Poland, Zygmunt Modzelewski, appointing me as representative of the Polish Press Agency, Polpress, for the whole of the Middle East! This meant a major stimulus to move to full legality and expand our work. I sent back to Modzelewski a list of our leading associates who were soon to take over the official representation of Poland in Palestine, until new consular staff could arrive from Poland.

I remained active in the Free Poland movement and the publication of our journal until 1947, when most of the Polish emigré community in Palestine and the Middle

East either went back to Poland or dispersed in the West. With the closing down of the journal, I was offered and accepted the post of a Consular and Press Attaché at the General Polish Consulates in Tel-Aviv and Jerusalem. A new stage of my activity opened. I never applied for, nor did I receive, any formal legal paper restoring my Polish citizenship which had been taken from me in 1938. I was simply issued first a service passport and then a diplomatic passport by the new Polish authorities.

Accepting a position in the Polish consular-diplomatic service was tantamount to a decision to return to Poland. I had few hesitations. Both ideology and expediency favoured such an option. Destiny. On the one hand, this meant a unique opportunity to participate in the socialist transformation of Poland, a historical turn in the expansion of socialism. On the other hand, there was a personal professional drive: the promise of a suitable job in an edifying position. It was indeed tempting.

Whatever hesitations I might have had were related to the nature of the communist regime in the Soviet Union. Realities in the Soviet Union under Stalin were not always commendable, and this I knew. My attitude to these realities had known cycles of enthusiasm and estrangement. I was enthusiastic about the October Revolution, which had given new hope for human liberation. But in 1937/38 I was taken aback by the Moscow trials, which seemed incomprehensible and repugnant. In 1938, I cut my contacts with the Communist circles in Danzig and joined the Zionist youth movement *Habonim* (The Builders). My refutation of Moscow's political behaviour turned into intense condemnation with the Molotov-Ribbentrop Pact. Was the Soviet Union following a socialist anti-fascist policy or pursuing imperial designs? Then, my confidence was somewhat restored when the Soviet Union acceded to the war against Hitler and started to play a paramount role in it. One indication of inner change in the Soviet Union was the appeal to national feelings and the formation of the Jewish Anti-Fascist Committee, which was now permitted to unfold a world-wide activity. Another sign of hope was the establishment of a formally independent Poland, with a separate state identity – contrary to communist revolutionary theory, which stipulated the incorporation of any newly liberated territory into the Soviet Union. Such designs – the notion of Poland as the 17th Soviet republic – had in fact been harboured in Moscow in 1942/43, sustained, among others, by Zofia Dzierżyńska, wife of the first Soviet security chief. But they were never to become reality. Though the shift to Polish independence took place under the special conditions after World War II, and under Allied weight, it was nevertheless a mark of a new orientation.

To me, it seemed hard to imagine that there could be a fresh relapse into mindless Stalinism. Well, like many other observers, I was wrong in my assessment, or rather, in my belief in the Soviet system. Still, my thoughts about returning to Poland were not all that free of concerns. In the mid-1940s, Poland was a constant battlefield, with the struggle between the nationalistic forces of yesterday and the new authorities who professed socialism and democracy. A heroic effort was initiated to rebuild the country from ruins, and the cream of the intelligentsia joined the new administration; but armed clashes between a right-wing underground and government forces continued. Nor was antisemitism a thing of the past. In July 1946, a pogrom in the city of Kielce left 42 Jews killed. Uncertainty was in the air. Thus, a return to Poland would mean both a willingness to take part in the reconstruction of

Poland, in rather difficult conditions, and to face the inevitable protracted strain. On the whole, however, it did seem alluring to be able to share in the remaking of the entire political and social system, under conditions of ascendant socialism.

At home, there was not full unanimity about moving to Poland. Erna, who had no Polish background, was rather sceptical. She instinctively feared this faraway country which was passing through a process of turmoil. Yet, finally she gave in, not wanting to stay in the way of my yearnings. Nor were we alone in choosing to return to Poland. Some of our closest friends, partly from among former members of the International Brigades in Spain, made the same decision. And general Jewish public opinion sympathized with the new Polish authorities, not least because of the active support that Poland had given to the Jewish national struggle in Palestine. Poland was among the first countries to grant diplomatic recognition to Israel, on May 18, 1948. And so, our decision was taken. Erna made a reconnaissance visit to Poland in 1948 and travelled to Warsaw in 1950 to give birth to our second daughter, Halina.

As it transpired, my duties as Consular and Press Attaché at the Polish Consulates in Jerusalem and Tel-Aviv were not without dangers. In 1947, I moved with my family to Jerusalem and had to shuttle between Jerusalem and Tel-Aviv. This became very risky, as Arab-Jewish military operations started at the end of 1947 and Jewish Jerusalem found itself under Arab siege. Our Consulate General in Jerusalem was located on the Arab side. To reach Tel-Aviv, I had to drive through Arab-controlled territories, over Ramallah, to the Jewish-controlled Lydda airport. From there, as the road between Lydda and Tel-Aviv was unsafe, I had to take an old Polish RWD single-seater plane to land at the Tel-Aviv stadium. To pass all the Arab and Jewish roadblocks and control-posts was a risky enterprise. Nor was I ever sure whether the wheels of the mini-plane would open for a safe landing. Later, when travelling between Tel-Aviv and Jerusalem, I took the so-called "Burma Road", an alternative track built by the Jewish resistance to bypass the Arab encirclement of Jerusalem.

As Press Attaché, I organized a regular information service providing Polish news for the local press, and sending back to Poland reviews from local journals, Jewish and Arab. Zuhdi Labib Terzi, who was later to become the PLO representative at the United Nations, served as my Arab translator at the Consulate in Jerusalem. In October 1949, I was promoted to the post of Consul in Charge of the Consulate General of Poland in Tel-Aviv. This was a very taxing position, comprising both administrative-consular and political-diplomatic work. The Tel-Aviv Consulate was the largest Polish consular office abroad: a substantial part of the Jewish population in Israel consisted of former Polish citizens, and there had been massive Jewish immigration from Poland following the establishment of the state of Israel. Then, I was also dean of a rather large consular corps in Tel-Aviv.

Parallel to my consular duties, I was also involved with work in the cultural and political domains. Responding to wide public interest, my Consulate organized various cultural gatherings and parties. Very often I was invited for lectures to collective settlements, the kibbutzim. I was especially proud to manage the publication of a luxurious edition of the famous Polish 19th century epopee of Adam Mickiewicz, *Pan Tadeusz*, translated into Hebrew by Józef Tenenbaum. I engaged myself personally both in stimulating the translation and in procuring high-quality wood-free paper, as

well as all the vignettes from Poland. I was also proud of having arranged the return
to Poland of the eminent lyrical poet and satirist Stanisław Jerzy Lec. Lec had been
Cultural Attaché in Vienna and deserted in 1950 to Israel. Later, however, he became
homesick and turned to me for help. Warsaw stubbornly opposed his repatriation. I
had to travel to Poland and intervene on the highest level for his return. Lec finally
went back to Poland, where he proved himself one of the most productive and imagi-
native poets, with many translations into foreign languages. At the same time, I had to
take charge of political and partly also of commercial Polish-Israeli relations. At that
time, Poland had no diplomatic representation in Israel, and diplomatic liaison was
entrusted to the General Consulates in Jerusalem (headed by Prof. Olgierd Górka,
the renowned Polish historian) and Tel-Aviv. As the seat of the Israeli Foreign Office
was then in Tel-Aviv, the bulk of the liaison fell on my Consulate.

Polish-Israeli relations were initially rather unproblematic. The Jewish national
movement and Israel were perceived as a power which, through its struggle against
the British colonial administration, forced open the imperial balance in the Middle
East. Poland evinced great interest in preserving Israeli neutrality between East and
West. But in the process, events began to move in another direction. From the early
1950s, for various reasons, economic and military, Israeli policy started to slide to
the West, mainly to the United States. This was not without consequences for Israeli-
Soviet and Israeli-Polish relations. They began to cool, and the chill reached our
Consulate as well. I became aware that, behind my back, one of my vice-consuls
had initiated intelligence activity. Polish foreign intelligence was at that time in its
infancy and, as far as I could gather, was rather groping about in the dark. I was
troubled: I could not do very much about it. Anyhow, I was then about to be recalled
from my position.

In August 1952 I was summoned back to Poland. This was rather a tense
period, with the Cold War growing stronger. The establishment of the Cominform
signalled the imposition of Stalinist dogma on the East European countries. In Poland,
following the suppression of the Gomułka national line in the Polish Workers' Party
and the incorporation of the Socialist Party into the Polish United Workers' Party,
the political atmosphere hardened. Antisemitism was on the rise both in the Soviet
Union and the East European countries. In 1948/49 the Soviet Union initiated an
ideological campaign against 'cosmopolitism' – which turned into the suppression
of Jewish cultural activity and resulted in the murder of leading Jewish intellectuals.
We were on the eve of the Moscow-staged "Doctors' Plot" and the Slánský trial in
Czechoslovakia. My colleague, the Czech envoy to Israel, Eduard Goldstücker, a
Jew, was in 1951 recalled to Prague, only to become implicated in the Slánský trial
and given a 10-year prison sentence.

For a moment I had second thoughts about my return. I decided, however, not to
disavow my superiors. My refusal to return could have been exploited to kindle anti-
Jewish feelings. But eventually, I myself fell victim of the rising tide of antisemitism.
Soon after my return to Warsaw, I was dismissed from the Ministry of Foreign Affairs.

2.4 Poland of "Real Socialism"

2.4.1 Waves of Antisemitism

I returned to Poland with my family in September 1952. We had thought of settling down in Poland for good, but the wheel of fortune was to shape things differently. With an interval of over four years in Indochina, where I served as member of the Polish delegation to the International Commission for Supervision and Control (ICSC) in Vietnam and Laos,[3] I stayed in Poland until November 1968. Then, we were virtually driven out of the country in the wake of consecutive antisemitic tremors.

With a time-lag of exactly thirty years, I was for the second time deprived of my Polish citizenship. However, in 1968 it was done in a different way: I was compelled, together with my family, to renounce citizenship before leaving Poland. Was there a line between the two incidents, leading from the 1938 administrative decision of the pre-war authoritarian Polish government to the behaviour of the post–World War II government of "real socialism"? However fundamental the socio-political transformation in Polish politics and the systemic metamorphosis from right to left, one component seemed to survive: the legacy of antisemitism.

Waves of antisemitism in post–World War II Poland appeared in cycles, abetted concurrently by policies of the Soviet Union and internal Polish inducement. The specifically Polish sway was driven by two complementary phenomena. On the one hand, right-wing anti-governmental circles, relying on the age-old conspiratorial theory that blames Jews for all evil, were at work to politically exploit the fact of the presence in the leadership of the ruling party of a number of Poles of Jewish descent. For them, antisemitism was a tool to spread mistrust and hatred of the Polish authorities. On the other hand, rivalry within the leadership of the ruling party trickled down to local levels and degenerated into perverse antisemitic postures. There was a mutual stimulation between both trends. They met and found rich nourishment in the traditionally prevailing vulgar antisemitism used as a scapegoat for all socio-political ills. The curious thing about post–World War II antisemitism was that, by then, the Jewish community in Poland had dwindled through the Holocaust from a figure of 3.5 million to some tens of thousands at most. In these circumstances, enduring antisemitism brought into focus its perennial utility as a scapegoat, playing on the deep-seated fundamentalist superstition and ignorance of large sections of the population.

At any rate, after my return to Poland I served a few weeks as senior councillor in the Independent Eastern Department of the Ministry of Foreign Affairs. In February 1953, as the fictitious Jewish "Doctors' Plot" in Moscow came to affect the Polish scene, I was discharged from the Ministry. I was in no uncertain terms made aware of the reasons why. I was invited to the Director of the Staff Department, Stefan Wilski, who seemed embarrassed as he tried to explain. He started by saying that the

---

[3] See Sections 3.2–3.4 and Chapter 5 below. (The editors.)

Ministry had no complaints about my work. On the contrary, I performed marvellously. Yet circumstances compelled the Ministry to act: "You should know better of the background". Wilski did his best to be polite and offered me help in finding another job.

I left the office of the Director in a state of mental agony. Was this then the true face of the communist system? The socialist promise of job security without discrimination had suddenly vanished. "Real socialism" seemed to be acting on different premises. In addition to practical daily worries about making ends meet, my life became desolate. For days and weeks on end I could not find a balance. It was obvious that in the prevailing atmosphere, with all institutions and enterprises under superior regulation, I would not be in a position to find a job, not even as a factory hand. There were rumours that a concentration camp was being prepared for 'cosmopolites'.

Eventually, however, a way out was found. I was transferred to the Polish Institute of International Affairs (PISM), a place of retreat for staff put aside by the Ministry of Foreign Affairs. Happily, soon after my transfer, on March 5, 1953, Stalin died; the "Doctors' Plot" was declared a sham; and a political thaw followed. In a way, chance cleared some of the clouds.

That meant I could begin to think of an endeavour which I had fancied for a long time: to complete my higher studies. Back in 1938, I had tried to enrol in Danzig at the Chemistry Faculty of the Polytechnical College but was not admitted on Aryan grounds. Now, I could use my relative leeway to realize my original intentions. This time, I was mainly interested in international relations. In the period between 1953 and 1966, parallel to my professional work, including partly my stay in Indochina, I gained three academic degrees: Magister in Journalism (1955), Dr. in Political Science (1959), and Dr. habil. in Contemporary History (1966). My doctoral thesis was entitled *The Near and Middle East 1945–1955: Rivalry between the Western Powers.* My Dr. habil. thesis was on *The Arab East: History, Economy, Politics.* Both studies were published in book form by the Publishing House Ksiazka i Wiedza (Book and Knowledge). In addition, I published a study in the book series of my Institute, *The Turbulent Laos: From the History of the Crisis 1954–1964.* Because of my previous connection with the Foreign Office, however, I had to sign all my publications with a pseudonym. I chose Marek Gdański, in token of my pre-war stay in Gdańsk (Danzig).

2.4.2   The Indochina Interlude

Soon after my transfer to the Polish Institute of International Affairs, I chanced to return for a short period to the foreign service – not as a career diplomat but to assist Polish diplomacy in its engagement in Indochina. Following the 1954 Geneva Agreements on Indochina, Poland, together with India and Canada, became a member of the International Commission for Supervision and Control (ICSC) in Vietnam, Laos and Cambodia. This was a demanding task. It required a large staff of competent and proficient experts in international relations, as well as knowledge of the diplomatic procedures and foreign languages – mainly English, the language of the Commission, and French, the lingua franca among government circles in Indochina. Each Polish delegation to the three countries of Indochina numbered at times up to 50–100 military officers and civilian staff.

In this situation the Ministry of Foreign Affairs offered me a position as councillor with the Polish ICSC delegation in Vietnam. Normal turnover of members of the Polish delegation was eight months. I stayed almost the whole of 1955 in Vietnam, first in Hanoi and Vinh, and then in Saigon, as head of the Polish delegation in South Vietnam. During this period, I established close personal relations with the Vietnamese liaison officers to the ICSC, quite beyond a dry diplomatic protocol. In Saigon I made friends with Pham Hung, the then chief of the North Vietnamese Liaison in South Vietnam and later head of the Vietnamese insurgency in the South until victory in 1975, and subsequently Vietnam's Prime Minister in 1987/88.[4] These relationships were to come to good use in the future.

Back in Warsaw, I returned to the Polish Institute of International Affairs. But in October 1956, chance unexpectedly played a role once more. The leader of the Polish delegation to the ICSC in Laos, Gen. Graniewski, became terminally ill. A replacement was urgently needed, someone able to handle the intricate situation in Laos. This was an unruly time in Warsaw, with the so-called Polish October in full swing. Following a deep crisis in the ruling party, Władysław Gomułka had been called to return to its leadership. Few people at the top had time to think about Indochina. The Ministry of Foreign Affairs needed somebody who knew the terrain, had experience of the work in the Commission and entertained good relations with the local parties. The Ministry was looking for a practitioner who could act independently and would not cause headaches in Warsaw. Apparently, I seemed a natural choice. And yet, when the Ministry proposed that I should take over the leadership of the Polish delegation to the ICSC in Laos, with the title of Minister Plenipotentiary, I could not believe that this was meant seriously. The appointment required a detailed screening by the Central Committee of the party, which I was sure I would never pass. But the Central Committee was in a state of disarray. Without any screening, and in great haste, I was provided with my appointment papers, a diplomatic passport and credentials to Laos, and then hurriedly sent through Paris and Saigon to Laos. As we flew over the Middle East, the stewardess announced the outbreak of fighting around the Suez Canal.

I was to stay in Laos until September 1957. There, I established cordial relations with the Pathet Lao leadership and sound cooperation with the parties in the Royal Government as well as the Vietnamese officers in charge of the Laotian affairs.

---

[4] In 1951, Phạm Hùng had been elected to the Executive Committee of the central committee of the Vietnam Workers' Party, the new name for the Indochinese Communist Party (founded 1930). Between 1952 and 1954, he served as deputy director of the party's Central Office for the Southern Region (known in English as COSVN). With the signing of the Geneva Accords in 1954, he moved to Hanoi, but returned shortly afterwards to Saigon where he worked as the head of the People's Army of Vietnam's High Command Liaison Mission to the International Commission for Supervision and Control. (The editors.)

At the same time, I also formed very friendly relationships with the other two Commissioners, Ambassador Samar Sen of India and Ambassador P.G.R. Campbell of Canada. Thanks to its cooperative spirit, the Commission was instrumental in the constitution of the first Government of National Union in Laos. (I presented a more detailed account of this period in my book, *Notes of a Witness: Laos and the Second Indochinese War*, published in 1973 by Random House, New York). Returning to Warsaw, I again went back to the Polish Institute of International Affairs.

Chance popped up anew in 1961. In 1958, following turbulent developments in Laos, the Laotian ICSC Commission was suspended. But in 1960, civil war broke out in Laos, and in April 1961 the Soviet Union and Great Britain – the two Co-Chairmen of the Geneva Accords – announced the reactivation of the ICSC. The conflict in Laos had become a cause of great international concern. Warsaw had to hurriedly establish a competent team for the Polish delegation. Taking into account my good record as Commissioner in 1956–57, the Ministry of Foreign Affairs proposed that I return to Laos. This time, however, I was told that I could not assume the leadership of the delegation. I was offered the post of the Deputy Chief, though I would retain the title of Minister Plenipotentiary. Personally, I was not very much concerned about rank, and accepted the offer. The work itself seemed alluring. My superior in Laos was Ambassador Albert Morski. We agreed on a division of labour: he remained in the capital Vientiane, in comfortable conditions; I settled down in the Liberated Territories controlled by Pathet Lao. Living conditions in the Liberated Territories were very primitive, but this was the place to build up close contacts with the Pathet Lao, the Neutralist faction and North Vietnamese. As time passed, Morski became increasingly frustrated by the complexities of Laotian-Vietnamese and Western policies. In May 1962, he returned to Poland. And so, Warsaw asked me to assume leadership of the Polish delegation. I stayed in Laos until January 1964, when I went back to the Institute in Warsaw.

2.4.3   At the Polish Institute of International Affairs

Apart from research at the Polish Institute of International Affairs, I became engaged in the Institute's monthly, *Sprawy Międzynarodowe* (International Affairs). At times I served as member of the Editorial Board, its Secretary and as Editor of the journal. I contributed a series of articles and reviews, mainly on problems of the Middle East and the Indochina conflict as well as Third World affairs. In addition, I published a number of articles on these issues in the theoretical monthly of the ruling party, the Polish United Workers' Party, *Nowe Drogi* (New Ways). At the Institute, I was working at the Asian Department, which I in fact headed in the final stage of my stay in Poland.

Looking back on my publications in Poland today, I feel rather ambivalent; both content and uncomfortable. On the one hand, my writing did maintain a rather good scholarly standard, well-documented and sound. On the other hand, it was tainted by the official policy in international relations, nor could it have been otherwise.

Ultimately, all studies on world affairs during the Cold War, East and West, bear the mark of the times. That said, I never ventured into internal systemic issues of "real socialism", but concentrated on international developments, mainly Middle Eastern and Indochinese affairs.

Middle Eastern problems have remained tangled to the present day. Issues of balancing the Arab-Israeli conflict always raise unanswered questions concerning the very dynamics of the conflict and the contradictory claims of the parties involved. Still, my book, *The Arab East*, retains lasting value. It has been well received in scholarly circles in the West as a factual historical and contemporary account. Left-Zionist publishers in Israel proposed a Hebrew translation. Similar suggestions for a Russian translation were turned down in Moscow – though the study was in fact unofficially admitted as a basic source material for Polish students at the Moscow University. At the Warsaw University, it became a standard component of the international curriculum.

In contrast with Middle Eastern problems, the Indochina conflict showed a more clear-cut historical profile. The US military adventure was certainly sickening, as well as being counterproductive to US interests. This was indeed an unjust war with dangerous international implications. Some insights on the roots of the conflict are offered in my book, *Notes of a Witness*.

2.4.4 Two Portentous Episodes

As it happened, my concerns in the two central fields of my studies – the Middle East and Indochina – in addition to my dissent through the Prague Spring of 1968 and its pursuit of "socialism with a human face", eventually contributed to my being banished from Poland in 1968. Two episodes related to the Arab-Israeli conflict and my stand on Indochina bring into relief my latent dissident position with respect to official Polish policy.

A moment of particular tension occurred in 1967, in the wake of the Six-Day Arab-Israeli war. It coincided with growing leadership rivalry within the ruling party, where strong antisemitic undertones became evident. On June 19, 1967, the First Secretary of the party, Władysław Gomułka, delivered a speech that was violently anti-Israeli and ostensibly antisemitic. Following the example of Moscow, Polish-Israeli diplomatic relations were severed. I was invited to the Propaganda Department of the party's Central Committee and asked to prepare materials branding Israel as a brutal aggressor. I responded by saying that what I could do was to compile a documentary record of events, unfolding the historical background and the immediate circumstances – political and military – which led to the outbreak of the war. These documents would then speak for themselves. My interlocutors were not happy, however. They would prefer a concise, one-dimensional, anti-Israeli documentation: a fabrication of documentary records. Eventually, they had to give in to my proposal. The publication was intended to reach the political leadership as well as party organizations. It was to serve as a basic source material.

In a very short time, I put together three volumes of original documents going back to the inter-war period, entitled *The Israeli-Arab Conflict – Selection of Documents and Materials*. The focus was on the course of events preceding the war, and the military-political behaviour of the main actors on both sides, their words and deeds. The collection included 296 documents, with the full text of pronouncements and declarations of the parties preceding the war. It also included a detailed chronology of events between 1947 and 1967, as well as a short factual political-economic survey of all states in the region. The three volumes were prefaced by an introduction, which I kept in a historical matter-of-fact style. To speed up production, the publication appeared in a duplicated form, with a circulation of several thousands, issued by the Documentary Centre of the Polish Press Agency in June and July 1967.

The publication of this compendium created a sensation among the Polish political and intellectual elite. It was the stuff which clearly contradicted the official version of events. A friend of mine phoned me to ascertain if I was not yet arrested. Others wondered how the materials had passed censorship. But the fact of the matter was that these volumes, being internal material, had never been submitted to the censors. Nevertheless, I did not escape trouble. In July 1967, *Nowe Drogi*, the theoretical organ of the party, published an article under my name, based on my introduction to the documentary compilation, with an addition – without my consent – of the most extreme excerpts from Gomułka's speech. After this, I vowed never again to write in Poland on Arab-Israeli affairs – a stand which I fully abided by. But I was not forgiven. One of the grounds for my expulsion from the party before leaving Poland, I was told, was that I had kept silent on Arab-Israeli affairs since the Six-Day War.

A more serious episode occurred in 1963, at the time when I was head of the Polish delegation to the ICSC in Laos. That country was then the focus of the Indochina conflict. The contest was in the process of expansion, with clandestine CIA operations pressing through Laos to the North Vietnamese and Chinese borders, using Meo[5] minorities as a base, and with the Vietnamese preparing the way to move through the Ho Chi Minh trail, across Laos, to South Vietnam. In Laos itself, the internal political and military battle had begun to escalate. After the assassination of the neutralist Foreign Minister, Quinim Pholsena, on April 1, 1963, the government of National Union was on the brink of disintegration. Historically, this was the opening period of the Second Indochinese War, on the eve of full US engagement in the war.

My position in the Commission was not an easy one. Since 1962, when I took over the leadership of the delegation, I had received almost no policy instruction from Warsaw. The Ministry of Foreign Affairs was satisfied that I had established correct rapports within the Commission and maintained good relations with the Laotians and Vietnamese as well as with the Soviet and Chinese ambassadors, and also with Western diplomatic representations. My internal compass had to take into account the position of the Pathet Lao and North Vietnamese, their political and strategic working assumptions. While I pleaded with them to pursue first and foremost political solutions, they believed more – in a realistic vein – in arriving at political solutions through military ascertainment and resolution. In this, both sides to the conflict

---

[5] Now normally referred to as Hmong. (The editors.)

seemed to meet, and an atmosphere of war prevailed. Nor was my position made any easier by the growing rift between the Soviet Union and China, with clear political and military implications for the ongoing struggle in Laos and Indochina. Also, here I had to try and balance all the conflicting interests, with all the three great powers – the United States, China and the Soviet Union – actively involved in the conflict.

The paramount danger, as I saw it and as history proved it, lay in the intensification of US military intervention. An active arm of this intervention in Laos was the paramilitary organization 'Air America', which airlifted supplies for the Meo units behind the Pathet Lao positions. As the struggle for the key strategic site in central Laos, the Plain of Jars, intensified, Air America assumed transport of the right-wing troops of Gen. Nosavan from Vientiane to the Plain of Jars. On April 26, 1963, 17 Air America planes landed with troops and supplies on the Plain of Jars. By chance, the three Commissioners – the Indian Ambassador, Avtar Singh; the Canadian Ambassador, Paul Bridle; and myself – happened to witness this activity of Air America on the airfield of Vientiane.

I was deeply worried by the aggravation of the crisis. I spoke to the US Ambassador, Leonard Unger, trying to draw his attention to the looming dangers of a protracted war. I pointed to the experience of France, which had lost a lengthy war despite knowing the terrain well after a hundred years of colonial rule. But Unger was not convinced. His answer astounded me: "How can you compare the United States to France: the US is a great power". Pure arrogance of power! I then tried to activate my two colleagues in the Commission to undertake some concrete action to restrain the activities of Air America, but to no avail. The Indian Commissioner did not conceal that, for him, instructions from New Delhi took precedence. And India was in conflict with China: this determined India's attitude. At the same time, the Canadian Commissioner admitted that, for Canada, what was decisive was the position of the United States. He himself had to coordinate all his steps with the US embassy in Laos.

Foiled in my attempts to win my colleagues in the Commission over to a concerted action against further US military involvement in the conflict, I thought that at least a way should be found to alarm international opinion of the perils ahead. The course of the conflict in Laos was little known in the outside world. Everything seemed hidden in the jungle. So, on April 28, 1963, I called a special meeting of the Commission and delivered a statement on the acute hazards of the situation. Not getting a positive response from the Indian and Canadian Commissioners, I demonstratively left the meeting. This was perhaps a diplomatic misstep. In my absence, the remaining two members of the Commission tried to turn the argument around, charging the Polish delegation with lack of willingness to restrain Pathet Lao military operations.

The affair resulted in an international outcry, with the USA threatening Poland with economic sanctions. Under the title "U.S. Using Trade Weapon to Sway Poland on Laos", E.W. Kenworthy reported in *The New York Times* of May 18, 1963, that Assistant Secretary of State William R. Tyler had had several conferences with the Polish Ambassador, Edward Droźniak, warning him about the consequences in US-Polish relations because of the behaviour of the Polish Commissioner, Marek Thee. Soon afterwards, in an editorial under the title "Polish Sabotage in Laos", *The New*

York Times wrote on May 21, 1963: "The United States has warned Poland that Thee's conduct is arousing such resentment here as to imperil President Kennedy's effort to lift the recently established trade barriers against Poland".

Warsaw was dismayed. The Deputy Prime Minister in charge of Economic Planning, Stefan Jędrychowski, was reported to lament that "because of Marek Thee, Poland will not receive the vitally needed grain". After a long period of no instructions from Warsaw, I suddenly received a ciphered message ordering me to come to Warsaw for clarification.

I arrived in Warsaw on Saturday, May 25. Following initial talks at the Ministry of Foreign Affairs, I was directed to Zenon Kliszko, the second in command of the party after Gomułka. I began by trying to explain to him the motives behind my action. I pointed to the convolution of the situation in Laos, emphasizing the dangers of a major military conflagration. World peace seemed to me threatened. Kliszko listened attentively but did not seem impressed. After a while, he said: "But Cde. Thee, you have to understand that grain is for us very important, more than the conflict in Laos". I was puzzled. Particular national interests, rather minor in relation to world peace, were considered more important than international solidarity and the struggle going on in Indochina!

I left the office of Kliszko rather confused. The Polish government wanted to heal the rift with the United States but could not fully disown the position taken by its representative in Laos. On May 29, 1963, the Polish Press Agency issued an official communiqué declaring Poland's willingness to join in the establishment of peace in Laos. The communiqué defended my stand in the Commission, saying that "The Polish Representative aims at concerted cooperation with the other members of the Commission in order to implement the Geneva Agreements and to help the Laotian Government in overcoming the arising difficulties and in the normalization of the situation".

There were rumours in the West, noted particularly in the Bangkok papers, that I would be held back in Warsaw and not return to Laos. But the decision in Warsaw was different. I was sent back to Laos to stay there until the end of the year. Then, after my return to Poland, I was told that my attitude to the Vietnam conflict and my assessment of its momentum were imbued by emotion and were naive. Especially my thesis that this conflict would not end until Vietnam could be united was challenged. "Vietnam will never be united", I was told. This stand was based on a nationalist, Eurocentric line of thought. Some circles in Poland feared that the unification of Vietnam might have an impact on the unification of Germany, which they shuddered at. In this respect, the Polish stand did not differ from the highly Eurocentric policies of the Soviet Union. From the 1954 Geneva Agreements onwards, the Soviet preoccupation with Vietnam and Indochina aimed at discounting their involvement for concessions in Europe, first in relations with France (aiming at the renunciation of the European Defence Community) and then with the United States (leading eventually to the 1975 Helsinki Accords on Security and Co-Operation in Europe, which was meant to confirm the post-Yalta borderlines in Europe). In a sense, then, the divergencies of views between the Polish authorities and myself reflected a clash between a narrow nationalist-great power orientation and an internationalist perspective focused on global progress and peace.

The above two episodes concerning the Arab-Israeli and Indochinese conflicts had led to a latent, smouldering conflictual situation between me and my superiors. It burst into the open in the spring of 1968, with my support for the Prague Spring. This, compounded by the resurgent antisemitic wave, meant that I was forced to flee Poland with my family.

2.4.5   The Prelude to Expulsion

The spring 1968 upheavals, which in the historical Polish parlance became labelled "the March 1968 occurrences", did not come suddenly out of the blue. Their anti-semitic tenor lay in the intensification of the inner struggle for leadership in the ruling party of Poland, Jews being anathematized as the conspiratorial hand at its top. The two contenders for the First Secretary post held by Władysław Gomułka were the Minister of Interior Mieczysław Moczar and Silesian party boss Edward Gierek. Especially Moczar was behind a vile chauvinistic antisemitic campaign that had lingered on since the mid-1967 Six-Day War antisemitic outburst.

Moczar's campaign brought into the open a nationalistic policy line of the ruling party that had continued with growing intensity since "real socialism" took over power in Poland. Excess in nationalist propaganda was part of the party's conscious strategy to win credit in the Polish society, which historically was characterized by profound traditions of nationalism. In the process, nationalism grew ever stronger, institutionalized by the powerful centralized bureaucracy.

Yet the deeper roots of the spring 1968 upheavals lie in the convergence of three dissident currents that had been growing parallel to the failure of "real socialism" and were eventually – 20 years later – to bear fruit in its final downfall. First was the socio-economic and political discontent with a system that had proved unable to deliver the material and civilian goods promised by "real socialism". Then came the cultural-intellectual tension resulting from the fetters and censorship imposed on all works of art. Finally, there was the upsurge of national sentiments in protest against the official policy with its Moscow orientation. All these currents got a powerful stimulus with the eruption of the Prague Spring professing "socialism with a human face" and the January 1968 election of Alexander Dubček as First Secretary of the Czechoslovak Communist Party.

It was no coincidence that the first symptoms of unrest became manifest in student demonstrations in December 1967 at the new staging of the 19th century play by Adam Mickiewicz, *Dziady*, based on an ancient folk-ceremony of calling forth the ghosts of the dead. In its original version, the play had contained clear anti-Tsarist pungency. Now the student demonstrations gave to it a transparent anti-Russian and anti-Soviet meaning. In response, in January 1968 the authorities suspended the further performances of *Dziady*. This only embittered the student and intellectual community. Demonstrations followed at the Warsaw monument of Mickiewicz, and on February 29, 1968, the Warsaw Branch of the Writers' Union issued a strongly worded protest against the doings of the authorities.

In panic, the authorities brought in security phalanxes against the demonstrators. Repressive measures came to a head in March 1968 in the wake of continued demonstrations at the Warsaw University and other academic centres throughout the country. Students were beaten up by organized security squads, and massive arrests followed. On March 19, 1968, Gomułka delivered a tough programmatic speech accusing leading intellectuals and professors at Warsaw University (including the well-known philosopher Leszek Kołakowski) of hostile, anti-socialist and 'revisionist' views, and of instigating "factious actions" by the students. His key point was that the student leaders were of Jewish origin. He then divided Jews into three categories: 'Zionists', 'cosmopolites' and true Poles, and called on the 'Zionists' and 'cosmopolites' to leave Poland. The expulsion order was thus given.

Soon afterwards, "anti-Zionist" mass meetings were orchestrated in all state institutions and factories, and resolutions adopted with unequivocal antisemitic undertones. Subsequently, hundreds of leading intellectuals, university professors and employees of central institutions were dismissed from their jobs. The atmosphere was one of intellectual terror. It was anybody's guess where this mad psychosis could lead. Even those who intended to leave the country were not sure of their fate. Eventually, a mass exodus ensued, comprising in the years 1968–70 over 20,000 people.

However, not all yielded to this moral insanity. There were examples of courageous resistance even on the highest levels of the ruling party. On March 20, 1968, when an 'anti-Zionist' resolution was tabled at the staff meeting of the Ministry of Foreign Affairs, the Minister of Foreign Affairs, Adam Rapacki, who was also a member of the Politburo of the party, demonstratively left the meeting, never to return to his office again. Also, Edward Ochab, a former First Secretary of the party, protesting vigorously against the antisemitic campaign, submitted his resignation from the Politburo and from the post of Chairman of the State Council.

I did not participate in student demonstrations or in the protests against the banning of *Dziady*. But at the Institute, my position was well known. I sharply criticized the "anti-Zionist" resolution tabled at the staff meeting of the Institute and abstained demonstratively when it was put to a vote. For this cardinal sin I was later repeatedly reproached. Furthermore, I came openly out in support of the Prague Spring. I was summoned before the Executive Committee of the Institute's Party Organization for a regular interrogation on my political leanings. Topping all the 'offences' were my "nationalist-Zionist" views. Consequently, procedures were initiated for my expulsion from the party, as a start for further reprisals. These included my dismissal from the Institute.

2.4.6 The Kafkaesque Trial

The proceedings for my expulsion from the party unexpectedly turned into a some-what protracted process. Initially, the Executive Committee was unable to mobilize a majority vote for its motion. One of the circumstances was the fact that, apart from being an independent scholar with a considerable creative output, I was also Chairman of the local Trade Union Branch, the only elected position at the Institute. As head of the Trade Union Branch, I was in a position to extend help to some members of the Institute who experienced acute socio-economic predicaments. The Executive Committee tried to manipulate and misrepresent this as one of my great transgressions. In particular, I was accused of having promoted a financial allowance to Mrs. Modzelewska, the wife of the prominent dissident Karol Modzelewski, despite the fact that – as maintained by the Executive – her husband "refused to accept productive work" as offered by the authorities. Nobody took such arguments seriously, however.

But the party had to win the battle. The final meeting at which I eventually was expelled from the party took place on April 11, 1968, lasting late into the morning of April 12. It was something straight out of the Middle Ages catechetical trials. The charges against me included such bizarre dogmatic reproaches as "the true error of Cde. Thee consisted in giving precedence to cold scholarly reasoning before polit-ical judgement" (Cde. Tadeusz Bratkowski), or "there is no time now for scholarly intellectual speculations" (Cde. Skiba). Still, until late into the night the Executive Committee was unable to force through its motion. It then resorted to the help of the Deputy Director of the Staff Department of the Ministry of Foreign Affairs, Cde. Kazimierz Ciaś.[6]

Cde. Ciaś arrived at midnight, armed with a thick confidential volume of my personal files. This included hundreds of denunciations covering my professional activity, from Palestine and Israel up to Indochina and Poland. I had always been aware that denunciations against me abounded: this was part of the system. But suddenly I realized that whatever I did and wherever I was, I was surrounded by a net of security agents and eager informers, each trying to outdo the other in painting a most wicked image of me. And yet, in his presentation, Cde. Ciaś managed to surpass anything I could possibly have conceived of.

Cde. Ciaś started by saying that, though the meeting was to deal with the case of Thee, few were aware of my real identity. Thus, "Thee was Polish Consul in Israel and had contacts with Zionists ... Thee was Polish Representative in Indochina and had contacts with the American Embassy and the CIA". I was flabbergasted, unable to believe my senses. Was the performance of Ciaś the figment of his own imagination? Or was it part of a well-shaped scenario imposed from above? This was an unreal farcical world all too reminiscent of the methods of the Inquisition. It brought to my mind *The Trial* by Kafka. And thinking back on the fate of Eduard Goldstücker, the Czech envoy to Israel, who on similar charges was imprisoned in the course of the

---

[6] Kazimierz Ciaś, Head of the Personnel Department of the Polish Ministry of Foreign Affairs (1966–69) and secret agent for the Security Service. (https://pl.wikipedia.org/wiki/Kazimierz_Cia%C5%9B). (HT.)

Slánský Trial, I was almost sure that I would end up in jail, too. I found it useless to defend myself. What I did mention was that during my stay in Indochina one of my tasks was to entertain good relations with the Western diplomatic representations, and that I had sent to Warsaw hundreds of ciphered messages detailing the contacts and the information received. Actually, because of my strategic emplacement in Laos on both sides of the front, I became almost the exclusive source of information for both Warsaw and Moscow. In fact, while passing through Moscow in 1963, the Polish Ambassador complained that my messages coming via Warsaw took up a substantial part of his coding capacity.

Finally, Ciaś's threatening posture won the day. Opposition to my expulsion from the party was silenced. Early in the morning of April 12, 1968, the expulsion motion finally got through. But contrary to what the party zealots might have thought, I now felt truly relieved. When I left the meeting, breathing the fresh air of Nowy Świat Street, I recalled the inscription on the tombstone of Martin Luther King, "Free at last". My party chapter was definitely behind me. The shackles were gone. Still, a hard time lay before me and my family to win final freedom and find a new refuge abroad.

2.4.7   The World Behind the Iron Curtain

No one who has not lived through the daily trauma of "real socialism" – where, as Gorbachev pointed out in his June 1991 Nobel Prize address, "everything in the final instance has been determined by the use of violence" – can fully comprehend the world behind the Iron Curtain. It is almost impossible to grasp the omnipotent grip that the authorities had on the life of the society and the individual: their monopoly of power in everyday affairs, from work and housing, to food, health-care, school, and not least, intellectual activity. A systemic routine imposed itself on society and the body politics, depriving the individual of real choices. There was a dearth of even relative freedom to transcend the regime structures which conditioned human creativity itself.

Yet, not everything was black and white. There were moments of a thaw and semi-tolerance, as after the death of Stalin and during Khrushchev's first years in power. Such brighter times served to resuscitate hopes that eventually humanism might carry the day. It was at that moment that I published my book, *The Arab East*. But then again followed the curve of dogma and repression, making you doubt the chance of improvement and forcing you afresh to retreat into a shell of waiting for a new melting of the ice. Ultimately, given the systemic straitjacket, this was an unrealistic castle-building. Breaking out from this blind, mindless circle was almost utopian.

Especially in my case, because I had some insights into the making of foreign policy, it seemed unthinkable that freedom could be attained. Would the authorities ever let me go abroad with my family? When, in desperation, I eventually decided to leave the country and told this to my friends, they thought that I was daydreaming. The only outcome, they predicted, could be indefinite imprisonment.

I myself was full of scepticism and timidity. From April 1968 onwards, a large black car with two security officers, alternating every few hours, was parked before the house where my family and I lived. Its purpose was not fully plain to me: was it only intimidation, or a prelude to incarceration? The officers followed not only me but also my wife on shopping rounds. They did this not in a clandestine way but rather openly, as if to demonstrate that we were under surveillance. What I feared most was a police search of my flat. They could then find my private notes from Indochina which I had been psychologically unable to do away with or to endanger friends by hiding these notes at their homes. I had a very bad conscience because, by my conduct, I was also placing my family at risk. On the other hand, by now we were in the same boat anyhow.

2.4.8   Repressive Measures

In the meantime, as if on command, repressive measures followed, apparently aimed to drive me into a corner from which there was no retreat.

In mid-April 1968, I received a letter dated April 12, by which the publishing house Książka i Wiedza renounced the contract of September 1967 for a book on the conflict in Vietnam. At the same time, the publisher demanded that I repay the initial instalment of several thousand złoty, a large sum at that time. Was this meant to bind my hands?

On April 16, 1968, a letter signed by the Acting Director of the Institute, Mieczysław Tomala, discharged me from the position as Head of the Asian Department. Simultaneously, the Institute's monthly, *Sprawy Międzynarodowe*, withdrew my paper on Indochina, which had been announced for publication in the April issue. Instead, a violently "anti-Zionist" paper was inserted, written by the leading anti-Israeli expert, Tadeusz Walichnowski.

On April 24, 1968, all the Warsaw dailies published with great fanfare a communication by the Polish Press Agency heralding the exclusion from the party of a number of dissidents, leading intellectuals and state employees, mainly Jews. Among them was the father of Adam Michnik.[7] The names were systematically presented in alphabetical order, with mine the last on the list.

In a letter of May 8, 1968, the Headquarters of the Warsaw District National Council, responsible for housing matters, notified me that procedures had been initiated to evict me from my flat, on the grounds that I had been occupying, in addition to a living room and a bedroom, also a room specified for working purposes (my whole flat, including the office room, comprised 61.6 m^2). This threat was in pointed

---

[7] Adam Michnik (b. 1946) is a Polish historian, essayist, former dissident, public intellectual, and editor-in-chief of the Polish newspaper, *Gazeta Wyborcza*. (HT.)

contradiction to the law under which every "independent scientific worker" was entitled to an additional room for a home office. Of all measures undertaken against me, this was the most ominous. There was no free housing in Warsaw, and I could find no alternative place to live. Evicted from my flat, I could end up on the street or, in the best case, elsewhere far off in the countryside. This would mean an ill-omened exile. My family and myself were terrified.

The only person who might be able to help me out was the head of my respective department, the Minister of Foreign Affairs, since he was responsible for the allotment of additional working space for scholars attached to his department. How to complain to the Minister of Foreign Affairs, Adam Rapacki? I had no entry pass to the Ministry. But I did have a permit to the library of the Ministry, and this I used to go up to the office of Adam Rapacki. But on the door was a notice that Rapacki was no longer performing his duties. I felt shaky. Then, by chance, as I was descending the steps leading to the Foreign Minister's office, I encountered the newly appointed Deputy Minister of Foreign Affairs, Zygfryd Wolniak, who was also acting as Head of the department. Wolniak was an old acquaintance, as he had taken over my position as Consul in Charge of the Consulate-General in Tel-Aviv back in 1952. Now, his main task was to implement the purge at the Ministry. Yet he greeted me in a friendly way, and as if to show his goodwill and new power, he offered help. With a stroke of the pen, he repealed the order of the Warsaw District National Council Headquarters, reaffirming my right to additional working space in my flat. At Headquarters they were perplexed: was it possible to revoke an order given by the Security? But Wolniak knew well the limits of his authority. My case came to counterbalance the image of the man in charge of the purge. For the time being at least, I was rescued.

But the nightmare was not yet over. The key issue for my superiors, as it appeared, was to find some way to expel me from the Institute. From a purely legal point of view, this seemed beyond the bounds of possibility on two accounts: an "independent scholarly worker" could not be dismissed from his job, nor was the elected chairman of the local Trade Unions liable to be discharged. However, as it turned out, law counted little.

There was first the problem of getting the Scholarly Council of the Institute to agree to my expulsion. This required a flagrant violation of the law concerning scientific workers. But an escape clause was found. Article 26(4) of the law stated that "in exceptional cases the contractual relations can be abrogated in case the scholarly and research activities of the scholarly employee remain in crass contradiction to the tasks of the Institute or with the duties of the scholarly research worker".

Well, I was made to be the exceptional case. It could hardly have been easy for some members of the Scholarly Council to swallow the 'exceptional' formulation in my case. However, as I learned later, the vote was unanimous. Was the vote secret, I wondered, as the law would demand? At any rate, the members of the Scientific Council felt truly intimidated. One of the members of the Council came to me and tried to apologize for his vote: he feared there would have been consequences for him and his family had he not complied with the directive from above.

Then, in mid-July 1968, I was summoned to the Chairman of the District Board of the State and Social Workers' Trade Union, Jerzy Durajczyk. He chose to play with open cards. His argument went as follows: "It is true that the law concerning the status of independent scientific workers and the elected Trade Union chairman is on your side. On the basis of law, you cannot be dismissed from the Institute. Yet you should be aware of prevailing conditions. Today law counts for little. Even if you went to the courts, no law could protect you. Let's then make a deal: you leave the Institute of your own free will and I promise you to find some retreat. Of course, you cannot count on any alternative work in the domain of science. But you should be able to survive. Perhaps a job in the archives may be found." Pure lawlessness in action.

But this conversation with Durajczyk was helpful. I began to realize the dilemmas before me, including the opportunities inherent in my superiors' eagerness to get rid of me from the Institute in some settled way, circumventing the letter of the law. A gateway for leaving Poland with my family seemed to open up. I took up these issues with the Acting Director of the Institute, Mieczysław Tomala, and with the party Cerberus, Jerzy Prokopczuk. We soon arrived at a tacit accord. On August 1, 1968, I sent a letter to the Directorship of the Institute by which I consented to terminate my contract relationship "on agreed conditions". The cancellation period was set for six months, from September 1, 1968 to February 28, 1969. In response, I got a note dated August 31, 1968, signed by the Deputy Minister of Foreign Affairs (and former Director of the Institute), Adam Kruczkowski, dismissing me from the position of an "independent scientific worker" at the Institute with immediate effect. At the same time, the cancellation of the contractual relationship was suspended for six months.

The whole arrangement amounted to a sort of green light for my departure from Poland. For my part, I did everything to speed up my exit. In fact, I halved the cancellation period, and left Poland with my family at the end of November 1968.

2.4.9   Uncertainty and Hope

This period was a trying time indeed. One of my concerns was to find a suitable job abroad – no easy task at my age, nearing fifty. My preference was for peace research, where I could combine theory with a solid practitioner's international experience. At that time, there were two peace research institutes taking shape in Oslo and in Stockholm. Defying all bureaucratic and censorship codes, I sent to both these institutes open letters of application. In addition, taking into account my good relations with the Canadian colleagues at the International Control Commissions in Indochina, I turned to the Canadian ambassador in Warsaw, inquiring about the possibility of settling down in Canada. My friends in Warsaw were astounded by my behaviour. Sending letters of application abroad by open mail and contacting foreign embassies – these were considered sins which could not go unpunished by the Security.

However, my approach worked, and I got positive responses from all three countries. The Canadian Ambassador told me that Ottawa had granted my request and issued instructions to its embassy in Vienna to supply entry visas to Canada for my whole family. The Stockholm International Peace Research Institute, in a message conveyed through the Swedish embassy in Warsaw, expressed interest in employing me. However, as this Institute was in an early period of organization, I would have to wait some time. The most positive response came from Oslo. The Peace Research Institute, Oslo (PRIO)[8] happened to be looking for a suitable editor for a new English-language journal on peace designs. My qualifications seemed more than adequate. The Oslo response included both an entry permit to Norway for my whole family as well as an offer of immediate employment. It was thus the most attractive and I accepted it without hesitation. Good help in all the arrangements to move to Norway was extended by the then Director of PRIO, Johan Galtung, and his wife, Ingrid Eide, who by chance attended in autumn 1968 a sociological conference in Warsaw.

We had now arrived at the decisive moment. Would my agreement with the Institute in Warsaw work, and would the authorities let us go? The few months before leaving Poland were extremely nerve-racking, not least because of the uncertainty of the whole situation. On top of it all came bureaucratic formalities that were deeply humiliating. In order to get travel exit permits, my family and myself had to sign documents by which we renounced our Polish citizenship with no right to return to Poland. For me, losing Polish citizenship had by now become almost customary. Nevertheless, with my attachment to and faith in a democratic socialist Poland, this was a bitter pill to swallow. The travel documents expressly emphasized that the bearers are no longer Polish citizens – they are stateless persons with no right to enter Poland. Though it was public knowledge that we were moving to Norway, we had to sign a paper declaring that we were going to Israel. The packing crate, with the few belongings permitted to be taken abroad – household utensils, furniture and books – clearly addressed to Norway, was shown on the TV – accompanied by a comment that Jews are fleeing to Israel.

Packing was a time-consuming operation that demanded both physical and psychic exertion. Detailed typewritten lists had to be prepared. A numbered list of books in several copies had to be submitted to the National Library. University diplomas and 'antiquities' could not be taken abroad. In the last category were some of my cherished souvenirs from Indochina. Then came day-after-day proceedings in bitter cold at the railway customs station. Almost every book had to be examined in detail. To ease the process, the custom officers had to be bribed – my shipment agent told me that without a bribe I might well land in trouble. I thus settled the matter through his intermediary. It was actually the first time in my life that I had had to resort to bribery. All in all, this was indeed a nightmare. Looking back, I sometimes wonder how we could muster sufficient strength to get through this mental and physical pain.

Another aspect of taking leave from Poland was the inordinate financial costs, which I could cover only because I still had some savings from my Indochina tour of duty. I even had to pay for the renovation of our flat for the new tenants. I left Warsaw on November 29, 1968 – and was told to return my November salary. I had to cover the full costs of the state university education of my daughter, Maya. Then came the exorbitant packing and shipping costs, as well as the tickets to Norway.

---

[8] At the time, PRIO's name was International Peace Research Institute Oslo. In 2009, PRIO reinstated its earlier name, Peace Research Institute Oslo. (The editors.)

The atmosphere at home was indescribable. Our children, Maya and Halina, could not understand the sudden adversity, and felt extremely unhappy at having to leave behind their best friends. Maya was near to nervous collapse because of the way the university and the authorities treated her. In spring 1968 she had graduated as a Magister in English Philology. As a rule, each graduate was to take an 'aspirant' job at a place indicated by the university. But Maya was immediately told by the University Plenipotentiary Curator that according to new instructions she could not get a job teaching at a Polish school. Instead, she was directed to the Foreign Department of the Warsaw School of Statistics and Planning, which urgently needed a researcher with knowledge of the English language. Initially, the Staff Director was happy with Maya's skills. But when he got her papers and realized that she was born in Israel, he became pale in the face and sent Maya home. Maya was shocked.

Somehow, however, we survived. I left Warsaw by train for Oslo, and my family joined me three weeks later by way of Vienna, after I had made arrangements for their stay in Norway. Pain and sadness were in our hearts as we left Poland. Together with our friends who accompanied us to the railway station, we had tears in our eyes. Of course, we also felt sorrow for those left behind. But at the same time, hope and joy pervaded our souls. What would the future hold out for us?

Since then, I have pondered whether I should recount the circumstances and details of our exile from the Poland of "real socialism". What value do they have for posterity? However, I came to the conclusion that – perhaps more than through grand generalizations – history is laid bare through the particular, the specific, the personal. Only by examining the course of history as it affects individuals can we hope to grasp the whole situational context.

2.4.10   "Real Socialism" in Perspective

Looking back on my experience in Poland, I can at times take it as a kind of fortune, to have lived through the ins and outs of one of the main currents of contemporary history. It enriched my understanding of mankind and human society. Should I point to one predominant cause for the failure of "real socialism", that must be the lack of democracy, of openness, of pluralism and civil liberties. What was lacking was a democratic check-and-balance mechanism to correct what was so often invoked as the "errors and blunders" of the command system. This was especially felt in the economic domain, the centre of gravity of socio-political progress.

Moreover, paramount for the systemic and economic decay was the subordination to the imperial policy of the Soviet Union, with the waste of a lion's part of resources and productive forces on a debilitating arms race with the industrially and technologically superior United States and the Western powers.

Essentially, the idea of socialism, as it emerged in the 19th and the dawn of the 20th century, was to initiate a novel experiment in conscientious human, socio-political and economic programming of human welfare. This requires civic autonomy, unobstructed initiative and participatory governance. It requires free interaction of the multitude of interest groups. It requires freedom of choices and freedom to speak out, as well as whistle blowing in case some of the adopted designs went wrong. To advance when the results met the expectations, and to retreat when the outcome proved mischievous. This kind of democratic flexibility was in dire want. Society was intimidated, and rarely did anybody dare to challenge the command economy and raise a critical voice. Once erroneous decisions were adopted at the top, they had to be implemented to the bitter end, until the whole system collapsed under the burden of totalitarian rule, economic retardation, wrong centralized decretory planning, wrong setting of priorities and wrong execution of even well-meant projects.

This fundamental imbalance between the democratic vision of socialism and its Stalinist implementation was compounded by the rigid ideological superstructure. "Real socialism" asserted an almost religious infallibility, aggravated by the centralization and monopolization of power. It imposed on society a uniform, fundamentalistic set of beliefs. It then arrogated the right to button up society into a straitjacket of mystic dogma, even by the use of extreme violence.

From the historical perspective, it was unfortunate that 'socialism', as envisioned by the idealistic thinking of modern philosophers, came to be launched not in a developed country with a sound economy and democratic traditions, but in a backward empire with byzantine authoritarian ways of governance. Actually, "real socialism" took over the worst of the past mode of political deportment of the previous regimes: dictatorship, oppression, chauvinism and the cult of the leadership. It stimulated nationalism despite being born under the banner of internationalism. It developed a system of arbitrary power and absolutism while professing freedom of the oppressed.

The experience of "real socialism" makes us aware of the detours of contemporary history. Seen in conjunction with the advances and retreats of the international society, with the shifting sands of war and peace, with the double-edged nature of science and technology – constructive and destructive, civilian and military – we arrive at a philosophical narrative of modern annals consonant with a non-linear, uneven, frail and sometimes erratic progression, rather than with a confident promise of fulfilment. History unfolds itself through clashes and mutual interaction between the rational and irrational, between continuity and discontinuity.

Can we attain a world order which would transcend the anarchic nature of contemporary international relations, aiming instead at a concerted undertaking for the establishment of non-violent, civilized, equitable and humane relations between nations, focusing on the betterment of the human condition? This is certainly a demanding bidding. The alternatives are between the consummation of the eternal brotherhood ideals of mankind on the one hand, and disorder and decay on the other hand. Overcoming the socio-political impediments to human fulfilment may for generations remain the conscientious historical responsibility of the individual and society.

2.5   The Indochinese Adventure

2.5.1   A Unique Experience

My triple stay in Indochina, in Vietnam and in Laos, was one of the most exciting and rich professional experiences in my life. First came Vietnam, where, in 1955, I served as Councillor of the Polish delegation to the International Commission for Supervision and Control (ICSC) in Vietnam with a seat in Hanoi.[9] Subsequently, I moved to Saigon as head of the Polish delegation to the ICSC in South Vietnam. My second term of duty in Indochina was in 1956–57, as Polish Commissioner to the ICSC in Laos, with the rank of Minister Plenipotentiary. And my third posting was again to Laos from spring 1961 to the end of 1964. Retaining the rank of Minister Plenipotentiary, I acted then initially as Deputy Leader of the Polish delegation to the ICSC in Laos, with a seat in the so-called Liberated Territories controlled by Pathet Lao/Neo Lao Haksat. From May 1962, I served as Polish Commissioner to the ICSC in Laos, with a seat in the capital Vientiane.

Indochina provided both a vivid adventure into the colourful and esoteric lands of South-East Asia as well as an education in the management and making of contemporary international relations. Moreover, as head of the Polish delegation, I had the opportunity to bring with me my family for short stays in Laos. We loved the excursions into the tropical green of Indochina, to the Red River and Mekong Deltas, to the plains and mountains of Laos, the Land of a Million Elephants. Again and again, we were spell-bound by the monumental temples and palaces of Angkor Wat and Angkor Tom, lost in the jungle of Cambodia. Emotionally moved by the subtle cultures and spiritual life of the Indochinese peoples, I pondered and tried to absorb the wisdom of Buddhism and Confucianism. We were touched by the gentle way of life of the Laotian people.

But more than anything else, my repeated stays in Indochina, during a period torn by great-power craft and war, served as a learning process on the course and tangles of global politics. Though fought in a limited area, consisting only of Vietnam, Laos and Cambodia, the protracted Indochina conflict was truly global in nature. It was the only political-military contest of the post–World War II period with the direct or indirect involvement of the big three – the United States, China and the Soviet Union. This was a conflict out of the ordinary, and it offered a unique opportunity for glimpses behind the curtains of diplomacy and strategy.

I found myself in the midst of the diplomatic-military agitation, in on-going communication with the diplomatic community of East and West, at a time when

---

[9] The ICSC was set up to monitor implementation of the Geneva agreements of 1954. It consisted of delegations from India, Canada and Poland. As the Geneva conference had recognized three independent states in the former French Indochina (Vietnam, Laos and Cambodia), one ICSC was established for each of the three. Since the Geneva conference had divided Vietnam temporarily at the 17th parallel, the ICSC in Vietnam got offices both in Hanoi (North Vietnam) and Saigon (South Vietnam). As Marek Thee recounts, the ICSC in Laos received a new mandate under the new Geneva agreement on Laos in 1962. (The editors.)

the clash between the Russians and the Chinese was evolving. Simultaneously as I entertained close contacts with the warring Left, I was trying to activate the ICSC for the reduction of tension. All this was a singular experience indeed. I dare say that above and beyond my academic degrees and the acquired theory of international relations, Indochina served as grand field-study on the function and malfunction of today's international peace and war system.

Should I single out a few main lessons learnt and relearnt in Indochina, I would choose two. First, that great powers, irrespective of ideology or human protestations, essentially behave like great powers – bullying, domineering and imperious; and second, that a primary impulse for actions of great and small actors on the international scene, again irrespective of ideology and human protestations, is deep-seated nationalism, often cloaked under the ambiguous term "national interests". In no other Cold War conflict did ideology blur the underlying national issues so thoroughly as in Indochina. And yet, these behavioural traits of states and nations permeate international conflict and war situations, also today. A sound comprehension of international relations is hardly possible without seriously addressing these socio-political ills.

I have a feeling that we have still not sufficiently digested the lessons of Indochina. This is partly because research on the roots and dynamics of the Indochina wars was not given the required attention. Both France and the United States, suffering under the Indochina syndrome, preferred to put the residual trauma out of mind. The general impression from available US literature on the Vietnam War is that the lesson learnt by the Establishment boils down to an insufficient use of force (General Westmoreland, Henry Kissinger). Less thought is given to misconceptions, miscalculations and political blunders, and more to the technology of warfare, primarily the employment of military strength. When in 1984 I was serving as Hubert H. Humphrey Visiting Professor of International Studies at Macalester College in St. Paul, Minnesota, I was told by Asia hands at several US universities that funds for research on the Indochina experience were hardly available. The deficiencies of historical studies may be even greater in Vietnam, China or the former Soviet Union, not to speak about the complete absence of collaborative East-West studies on the Indochinese debacle.

We need not enter into great detail to apprehend that the two Indochina wars – France's "Dirty War" of 1946–1954 and the following US military entanglement that persisted up until the mid-1970s – mark a watershed in the 20th century history of conflict and war. During the course of these wars, the world's political-military landscape underwent a profound permutation. Seen in a broad historical perspective, the Indochina hostilities permeated and influenced almost all mainstream processes of international change during this century. They were part of the demise of the colonial and neo-colonial era. They reflected the rise and fall of the anticolonial revolution. They mirrored the post–World War II "manifest destiny" US drive westward to the shores of Asia, and its rebuff. They put in motion and largely shaped the triangular political-military dynamics between the United States, the Soviet Union and China, culminating in the US-China rapprochement and the process of US-Soviet détente in Europe, as well as the superpower arms control negotiations. They contributed to the break-up of the seemingly monolithic Soviet-Chinese Communist axis. And finally, as a key testing ground for the latest in military technology, Indochina introduced the concept of an "automated battlefield", adding further impetus to the shift in armaments from quantity to a race in military technology.

The gap between the obvious international consequences of the contest in Indochina and the dearth of efforts at a deeper scholarly insight into their background and momentum is truly astounding. The Indochina story deserves more attention from historians, politicians and society at large. There are lessons to learn.

I myself tried to summarize my experience in various publications.[iii] Here, I would like to note in addition a number of episodes which helped me to gain better insight into the course of events, and mention some issues related to the history and the outcome of the conflict. In particular, I would like to take up the enigma of Vietnamese nationalism and the paradox that Vietnam, although victorious, lost the fruits of peace, while remarking on the delusions of the US policy that brought the strongest world power into the quagmire of the Indochinese conflict and resounding defeat.

2.5.2   The Geneva Accords Defeated

One episode that stands out vividly in my memory concerns how the United States upset the 1954 Geneva Agreements on the restoration of peace in Vietnam. I arrived in Hanoi on a humid and rather cool February day in 1955. The ICSC in Vietnam was then busy trying to implement the Geneva Accords, particularly the effectuation of the ceasefire, the supervision of the "freedom of movement" clause and the prevention of reprisals and discrimination against persons or organizations on account of their activities during the hostilities. Our main attention and concern were oriented towards implementing the provisions of the Final Declaration of the Geneva Conference, which stipulated that political problems were to be settled "on the basis of respect for the principles of independence, unity and territorial integrity" of Vietnam. To this effect, the Declaration provided for general elections to be held in July 1956 on the whole territory of Vietnam under the supervision of the ICSC, with consultations on this subject to start between the representatives of North and South Vietnam on July 20, 1955.

At the ICSC, we were well aware that the United States and their man in Saigon, Ngo Dinh Diem, were opposed to the elections that were meant to result in the unification of the country. It was generally assumed that Ho Chi Minh, hero of Vietnamese independence, would emerge as the unquestionable winner. We studied the roots of the US involvement going back to the "loss of China" syndrome, Cold War policies and the massive support for the French war effort. Still, we cherished the hope that what would prevail would be a peaceful solution on the lines stipulated by the Geneva Agreements, solemnly accepted by East and West, and providing for the unification and neutralization of Vietnam. But as political realities unfolded, these hopes dwindled into scepticism.

On July 20, 1955, the first anniversary of the Geneva Accords, we were shocked by mass demonstrations in Saigon against the Geneva Agreements. Organized and orchestrated by the Diem administration, they heralded a collision course with whatever was agreed in Geneva by the major powers and the local parties. Thousands of demonstrators marched through the streets of Saigon with banners condemning the Geneva Accords and abusing the ICSC. The fury of the marchers was directed particularly against the compounds of the ICSC and the Saigon office of the North Vietnamese Liaison Mission.

I was then staying in Saigon, residing with other senior members of the ICSC at the Hotel Majestic. A large mob armed with stones, knives and hatchets arrived in front of the hotel, shouting and yelling slogans against the ICSC. It was terrifying. I felt as if a massacre were imminent, and recalled the 1952 Black Saturday in Cairo, in the course of which hundreds of Europeans had been slaughtered.

With no police in sight, the building was soon stormed and wild wrecking of the hotel and its furnishings started. The noise and pandemonium in the corridors were horrifying. We could hear panic-stricken screams from the entourage of US Senator Perle Mesta. In no time, the mob moved to charge the rooms of the Commission members, and before long I heard axes hammering on the solid wooden door of my suite.

I was not alone in my room. With me was an elderly friend, Deputy Leader of the Polish delegation to the ICSC in Hanoi, Tadeusz Perl. Both of us realized the gravity of the situation. Would we survive? We prepared for the worst and bade each other farewell, promising each other to convey greetings and love to our families, should either of us remain alive. I hid in a large wooden wardrobe, but my friend stayed seated in an armchair, unable to move. Suddenly, with a bang, the door was smashed, and a gang of frantic youngsters invaded the suite. Looting seemed to be topmost in their minds and they turned straight to the cupboards. Through an opening in my wardrobe, I spotted my friend, taking advantage of the commotion, who stood up and, gathering his nerve, left the room. Then it was my turn. A youngster with a hatchet in his hand leapt to my wardrobe and threw open the door. But evidently, aghast at finding a living human being before him, he slammed the door and ran to other cabinets. The preoccupation of the mob with plundering and looting, in all likelihood, saved our lives. It was all over in a flash. Soon, French military units, still stationed in Saigon, arrived to lead us to safety. I left the hotel in shorts only, carrying no personal effects, only the hotel key in my hand. Indeed, the ornamented key of room 208 of Hotel Majestic remains a cherished souvenir from my Indochinese adventure.

One offshoot of the 1955 Saigon upheavals was the tightening of bonds of friendship with Pham Hung, who then headed the North Vietnamese Liaison Mission in Saigon. He found himself in the same predicament as the ICSC, facing a threatening mob which surrounded his compound. He managed to escape and turned to me for protection. I may say that I saved his life. Pham Hung was a Southerner, high in the hierarchy of the Communist Party. He was born in the Mekong Delta and in 1931, as a young revolutionary student, he was arrested and condemned to guillotine; this sentence was commuted to life and Pham Hung spent fourteen years in prison. The mastermind behind the insurrection against the Saigon authorities, and its leader between 1967 and 1975, he was later to serve as Deputy and Acting Prime Minister in Hanoi. In 1987, Pham Hung replaced Pham Van Dong as Prime Minister. He then invited me to come to Vietnam, but while I was making preparations to leave in spring 1988, he died.

Pham Hung always remembered the Saigon episode. Whenever I visited Hanoi, during my stay in Laos, he would receive me cordially and offer me opportunities to meet and talk to people in the Vietnamese leadership. For much of my insight into the course of events and the mindset of the Vietnamese, I am indebted to the friendship with Pham Hung.

The July 1955 Saigon demonstrations were clearly part of the US design to torpedo the Geneva Agreements. The United States was nervous about the possible outcome of nationwide elections in Vietnam: the prospects were that 80% of the Vietnamese would have voted for Ho Chi Minh.[iv]

In an assessment of US policies, *The Pentagon Papers* – the US Defense Department History of US Decision-making in Vietnam – maintained that the United States viewed the Geneva Accords as a 'disaster' and assumed "a direct role in the ultimate breakdown of the Geneva Settlement".[v]

The US design, orchestrated by the US Secretary of State, John Foster Dulles, was not for a political but for a military solution. As outlined by Dulles in a confidential conversation with the British Foreign Secretary Anthony Eden, the aim was "to hold some sort of bridgehead [in South Vietnam], as has been done in Korea until the Inchon landings could be carried out … this meant that things would remain on the boil for several years to come …".[vi]

2.5.3   The Two Governments of National Union in Laos

My second and third stays in Indochina coincided with the aftermath of the breakdown of the Geneva settlements. In line with the Dulles design, the conflict had become militarized, with Hanoi in the process impelling the insurgency in South Vietnam. The centre of gravity of the conflict moved to Laos, adjacent to North and South Vietnam. In a turbulent atmosphere of military coups and countercoups, a struggle evolved around the implementation of the Geneva Accords concerning Laos.

At issue was the problem of national reconciliation between the right-wing Royal Government on the one hand, controlling 10 provinces of the country and acting under the "protective umbrella" of the South-East Treaty Organization (SEATO), and the Left Pathet Lao/Neo Lao Haksat on the other hand, controlling two provinces in the North and enjoying the support of Hanoi.

Taking advantage of the growing unrest, North Vietnam had built up a sophisticated secret supply net linking Hanoi with the uprising in South Vietnam. The famous Ho Chi Minh trails running through Laos, by-passing the fortified narrow belt of Central Vietnam, came into being. Twice in this period, in November 1957 and June 1962, subsequent to convoluted negotiations, the parties in Laos were led to form a government of National Union aiming at accommodation and neutralization of the country. In these efforts, the ICSC in Laos played a supportive role, and I can recall with satisfaction my personal contribution to these agreements.

In spring of 1957, negotiations for the formation of a coalition government met with the disapproval of the Western powers. Pressures against the establishment of a government of National Union were mounting. I then, along with my colleagues in the ICSC, the Indian Chairman, Ambassador Samar Sen, and the Canadian Ambassador P.G.R. Campbell, started a discussion of how the ICSC could help to overcome these adversities. Consequently, it was on my initiative, as noted in the report to the Co-Chairmen of the Geneva Conference, that the Commission adopted a resolution which proved beneficial for the pursuit of the negotiations between the parties. In this resolution, dated May 16, 1957, the Commission "notes with concern and regret from its study of the situation that the Parties had encountered difficulties of various kinds, so that they have not been able to achieve a final settlement as foreseen in the Geneva Agreement". The resolution further stressed the Commission's view "that the Parties should remain free to discuss and determine between them what is most equitable and acceptable". The Commission then recommended "that the negotiations now in progress ... should be continued with the utmost vigour in the atmosphere of existing goodwill and mutual understanding until a final settlement on all outstanding points is reached with the least possible delay".[vii]

The wording of the resolution was well taken and made an impact on the parties. On May 29, the National Assembly ratified the agreements thus far signed. Though the crisis in the negotiations still persisted for some time, ultimately, the Commission's stand had its effect, and in November 1957 the first Government of National Union came into existence under the leadership of Prince Souvanna Phouma.

However, this government was not to last long. It survived only eight months. As recalled by Prince Souvanna Phouma on June 14, 1962, at the plenary session of the Geneva Conference on Laos, the US threat to cut off aid to Laos provoked his resignation in 1958. The subsequent government of Phoui Sananikone – Prince Souvanna Phouma noted – "clearly deviated from the road of neutrality and adopted a pro-American policy. To begin with, he permitted the United States to install American military advisers and instructors in our country ... What was graver, he introduced a policy of discrimination toward the Pathet Lao, and placed its leadership in prison, despite the fact that several were members of the National Assembly. All this revived the civil war ... In December 1959, a coup d'état brought to power extreme elements of the army [led by Gen. Phoumi Nosavan] ... These violations of the elementary rights of the people and other acts of injustice provoked the coup d'état of August 9, 1960 [led by Captain Kong Le] which faithfully reflected the aspiration of our people for a life in peace and general concord."

In 1958, under US pressure, the ICSC was requested to leave Laos. But then the civil war grew in intensity, impelling the reactivation of the Commission in spring 1961. Simultaneously, the two Co-Chairmen of the 1954 Geneva Conference, Great Britain and the Soviet Union, extended an invitation to all great powers, the United States, China and France included, to all neighbours of Laos and to the three members of the ICSC to a conference on the settlement of the Laotian problem, to be convened in Geneva on May 12, 1961.

The ensuing period was highly precarious and stormy. The Geneva Conference on Laos, which was supposed to arrive at a settlement in a matter of weeks, went on until July 23, 1962. Its outcome was an impressive Declaration on the Neutrality of Laos. But in the meantime, while negotiations in Geneva and Laos were initiated, the military contest continued, with the insurgency in South Vietnam on everybody's mind. Both the United States and Hanoi saw all of Indochina as an inseparable strategic battlefield, in which Laos was but a momentary focal point. On March 23, 1961, US President Kennedy devoted an entire press conference to the Laotian crisis, defining it "as the most immediate of the problems that we found upon taking office". While paying lip-service to a peaceful solution, all parties sought to achieve the military preponderance they considered decisive for the outcome of the struggle. On the one hand, pursuing a shift in force relations, Hanoi was bent on a protracted guerrilla military confrontation. On the other hand, the United States was preparing for a long-term counterinsurgency battle, perceiving the Indochina contest as critical in stemming the assault of global Communism. As negotiations for a political solution in Laos dragged on, the parties seemed more interested in keeping the conflict in flux until one or the other side could gain the upper hand militarily.

In this complex situation and following the strategic concept of advancing on two feet, military and political, the parties in Laos moved to the formation of the second Government of National Union. I followed the negotiations closely and, hoping for lasting solutions, tried to expedite their success. On June 12, 1962, a preliminary agreement was signed on the Plain of Jars. But hesitations and controversies on the composition of the government as well as on the mode of its functioning continued. There was a danger that the initial accord might wear away. To save the Plain of Jars agreement, I felt I had to step in.

On June 20, 1962, I organized, at short notice, a working lunch in honour of the Prime Minister designate, Prince Souvanna Phouma. I invited the Indian and Canadian Commissioners, the ambassadors of the United States, Great Britain and France as well as the Soviet Chargé d'affaires and the Foreign Minister designate, Quinim Pholsena. After my toast to the success of the mission of Prince Souvanna Phouma, a long exchange of views followed. The Prince was first to express his gratitude for the opportunity to gather support for his assignment. Speaking of the prevailing difficulties, he appealed to the ambassadors for a last try to save the negotiations. In question was the resistance of the head of the right-wing forces, Gen. Nosavan, whose position had been hardened by the resumption of US military aid. The main speaker was the French ambassador, Pierre-Louis Falaize, who in diplomatic language but with unmistakable reference to the nature of the impediments called for a cooperative effort to return to the Plain of Jars accord. Discussions lasted three hours. When the guests left my residence, the general feeling was of relief and of an improvement of the chances for finally achieving a Government of National Union. And indeed, this did come to fruition, not least thanks to an interposition made by the US ambassador, Winthrop G. Brown. The second Government of National Union was formed on June 23, 1962.

However, my hopes of a lasting solution were not to materialize. Any such solution depended on a parallel denouement of the question of South Vietnam. This was not to be. Instead, military operations in South Vietnam escalated. The agreement on the neutrality of Laos, so solemnly arrived at in Geneva, was violated by the warring parties, and the Government of National Union in Laos disintegrated. The Laotian crisis was to prove but a prelude to the Second Indochinese War with its massive US military engagement.

2.5.4   The US-Indochinese Engagement

How did it all come about? Ever since the mid-1940s, when the USA became involved in supporting the French colonial comeback to Indochina, US motives had been of a strategic, global, Cold War and ideological nature, far transcending the issue of Indochina itself. A paramount factor since the Chinese Revolution was the US obsession with China. Vietnam was seen alternatively as the gate to or the vanguard of China. The China bogey started with the "loss of China" debate during the Truman administration and evolved in the context of Vietnam to a spectre of the "deepening shadow of Communist China over all of Asia", in the words of President Lyndon B. Johnson.

This China obsession was the more aberrant as it went against all sound strategic and geopolitical thinking. Years before the USA became involved in the Second Indochina War, just at the time of the conclusion of the 1954 Geneva agreements, when the fever for military bridge-building and "Inchon landings" in South Vietnam heightened in Washington, a group of military people led by General Matthew B. Ridgway, former commander in Korea and the Army Chief of Staff in 1954, rallying under the slogan "never again", had come out strongly against any China-targeted US military engagement on the mainland of Asia. In a sober memorandum to the Secretary of Defense, Gen. Ridgway emphasized that instead of an all-out anti-Chinese strategy, US policy should rather aim "to split China from the Communist bloc ... In fact, I would regard the destruction of such military power as inimical to the long-range interests of the US. It would result in the creation of a power vacuum in which but one nation could move, namely Soviet Russia... The statesmanlike approach would seem to be to bring Red China to a realization that its long-range benefits derive from friendliness with America, not with USSR...".[viii]

It took a long time, filled with military setbacks in Vietnam, until this strategic and geopolitical wisdom was finally assimilated by the US administration. At last, in the beginning of the 1970s, in an effort to gain China's goodwill for a disengagement from the Vietnam war, the Kissinger-Nixon policy managed to bring about rapprochement between the United States and China.

But US awakening to the realities of the Vietnam-China-Soviet relations came late in time. Only too late did the USA realize that its Indochina engagement was a wrong war, in a wrong place against a wrong enemy. Ho Chi Minh's Vietnam was long perceived as the precursor of China and the Communist bloc bent on spreading revolution in South-East Asia, with the neighbouring countries ultimately liable to fall like dominoes under the Communist onslaught. In fact, this was a gross misreading. One should recall the independent origins of the Vietnam Revolution, with the establishment of the Democratic Republic of Vietnam coming four years before the foundation of the People's Republic of China, with Ho Chi Minh repeatedly turning to the United States for help against the restoration of the French colonial administration, and of course the later Chinese-Vietnamese conflict. Clearly, to rate Hanoi as a simple stooge and agent of Peking and Moscow, consonant to the stereotype conspiratorial theory of world Communism, was to misunderstand the Indochinese political scene. The result was political confusion and strategic overreaction, leading to further escalation of the conflict. The US response to Hanoi's insurgency was amplified by aiming not at Hanoi only but at containing Peking and Moscow as well. And this then meant that the use of force would have to be augmented correspondingly.

I myself once experienced directly this overshooting of the mark. At a critical moment of the Laotian crisis, on April 21, 1963, a working lunch had been organized in Khang Khay, the seat of the Pathet Lao/Neo Lao Haksat headquarters, with the participation of Prime Minister Prince Souvanna Phouma; the Deputy Prime Minister and head of the Neo Lao Haksat, Prince Souphanouvong; the representatives of the Co-Chairmen of the Geneva Conference, the Soviet and British ambassadors; and the Indian and Canadian Commissioners, as well as myself as the Polish Commissioner. The discussion turned to the problem of placing a Commission team at the contested Plain of Jars. Initially, Prince Souphanouvong seemed inclined to favour this idea. Aware from talks in Hanoi of the categorical refusal of the Vietnamese, I was rather sceptical. In the following exchange of views, Prince Souphanouvong in fact shifted to my stance.

As was routine, the British and the Canadian ambassadors reported on the course of the discussion to the Americans. I later learned that this became the subject of considerations at the US National Security Council. The reasoning there ran as follows: if Prince Souphanouvong, initially agreeable to sending a Commission team to the Plain of Jars, subsequently, after the intervention of the Polish Commissioner, withdrew his consent, then the decision-power lies not with the local forces, but with Moscow and Peking, as represented by the Polish Commissioner! There would thus be a need to demonstrate Western military resolve strong enough to be appreciated in the capitals of China and the Soviet Union. The decision then was, as a warning and a threat, to show the flag in the Gulf of Siam and Thailand, on the border of Laos. Actually, in mid-May 1963, SEATO allies – Australia, New Zealand, Britain, Pakistan and the Philippines – were asked to send military units to Thailand, to join units of the US Seventh Fleet as well as US land and air forces dispatched there.

2.5.5 Misreading the Mind of the Adversary

The fallacious Cold War misconception of the nature of the Vietnam conflict deepened in spring 1961 as a result of an erroneous assessment in Washington of the Khrushchev-Mao relationship. This coincided with my second term of duty in Laos.

Contrary to the perception of the new US administration of President Kennedy, which thought in terms of a Chinese-Soviet monolith bent on expansion in Asia and the Third World, relations between Peking and Moscow were deteriorating sharply. Khrushchev's policy of peaceful co-existence with the West clashed with Peking's security concerns, which had been inflamed by US efforts to strategically encircle China, and particularly by its military intrusiveness in Indochina, on the "soft underbelly" of China. The November 1960 international gathering of the world's 81 Communist parties in Moscow did not solve these issues. In fact, it was to be the last such meeting of Communist parties in which the Chinese Communist Party participated.

The divergent policy orientations of Moscow and Peking came out into the open with a major ideological speech by Khrushchev on January 6, 1961. In it, in the aftermath of the international Communist council, he took a biting stand against the Chinese policy of inciting conflict with the United States. The main theme of his talk was "wars of national liberation". With a convoluted reference to Indochina, Khrushchev argued for caution and warned against hasty decisions and against instigating local conflicts in the name of national liberation. Such conflicts, Khrushchev emphasized, might lead to world war. But expounding his plea in the rift with China, Khrushchev used revolutionary language generally supportive of struggles of national liberation.[ix]

Unaware of the evolving policy clash between Moscow and Peking and apparently also not well versed in the doctrinaire communist theology and lingo, Washington misread Khrushchev's peroration. Contrary to Khrushchev's real intention, Washington interpreted this speech as Soviet-Chinese closing of ranks behind the Vietnamese insurgency, in an offensive endeavour to extend the mantle of Communism in Asia and the Third World, under the nuclear umbrella. Close associates of President Kennedy, the historian Arthur M. Schlesinger and Roger Hilsman in charge of the Indochina desk, recall in their memoirs the "conspicuous impression" Khrushchev's speech made on the new President. Kennedy "discussed it with his staff and read excerpts from it aloud to the National Security Council".[x]

Not comprehending the growing rift between Moscow and Peking, the final decision was to respond in force against the perceived Moscow-Peking axis: the far-reaching strategy of intense counter-insurgency in Indochina was born. The classic misreading of the mind of the adversary thus contributed to the kindling of the Second Indochina War. In a message to the Congress on March 28, 1961, President Kennedy emphasized his resolve "to prevent the steady erosion of the Free World through limited wars … Our objective now is to increase our ability to confine our response to non-nuclear weapons, and to lessen the incentive for any limited aggression by making clear what our response will accomplish".[xi]

And in a parallel secret "Program for Action for South Vietnam", approved by the President in April 1961, a set of detailed instructions was laid down for counter-insurgency operations, including "covert actions in the field of intelligence, unconventional warfare and political-psychological activities".[xii]

The long-haul military operations in Vietnam were put in motion. Even at a later stage, when there could be little doubt as to the rift between Moscow and Peking on questions of war and peace, and in particular on the course of war in Indochina, military operations that had been set in motion under varying labels of 'containment', 'pacification', "nation-building" and 'Vietnamisation' of the war could not be halted. As late as 1964, Secretary of Defense Robert McNamara, justifying the US military build-up in Vietnam, recalled Khrushchev's 1961 oration as "one of the most important speeches on Communist strategy in recent decades", requiring a forceful response.[xiii]

The US stand and the state of mind in Washington reflected an overconfidence in military might, coupled with a disregard for the resistance abilities of the adversary. Acting from a position of arrogance of power, the United States invested scant effort into gaining a deeper insight into the socio-political or even the geographical-climatic conditions of the battlefield in Indochina. There was little understanding of the fabric of the Vietnamese society, or knowledge of the historic background of the national liberation movement. Arrogance of power became a signal feature of the war, toughening the US propensity for a military rather than a political solution. In the process, the US got bogged down in a protracted guerrilla war and fell prey to a soul-searching, success-failure syndrome: the inability to grasp why there was only defeat while victory remained beyond reach.

2.5.6   The Soviet-Chinese-Vietnamese Controversies

I observed the course of events with dismay. All too clearly could I sense the policy divergencies between Moscow and Peking. They became evident from the first days of the ICSC return to Laos and the opening of the Geneva Conference in spring 1961. On April 25, 1961, on my way from Warsaw to Indochina to reactivate the work of the Commission in Laos, I participated in a briefing in Moscow for the leaders of the Polish delegation. The meeting, held at the Soviet Ministry of Foreign Affairs, was chaired by Deputy Foreign Minister Georgi M. Pushkin. He was visibly concerned to avoid a military confrontation with the United States and to arrive at a political solution as soon as possible. His instructions were for a prompt imposition of a ceasefire, and for the Commission then to supervise its strict implementation. In the meantime, he thought, the Geneva Conference on Laos would rapidly work out a general political settlement to the conflict. Pushkin envisioned that the Geneva Conference would be able to wind up its work within six weeks. Just as with the erroneous US assessments, this Soviet scenario for a prompt solution reflected a similar lack of in-depth knowledge of the field realities in Indochina.

Two weeks later, when the Chinese delegation to the Geneva Conference, headed by Deputy Premier and Foreign Minister Chen Yi, arrived in Moscow en route to Geneva, it presented an entirely different scenario. I learned that Chen Yi considered conditions in Indochina not yet ripe for stabilization or a final settlement. The progressive forces in Laos had gained great victories, but those victories, he argued, were not yet solid, and the United States was not yet reconciled to defeat. There was thus a need for a protracted struggle, alternately employing forms of political and military combat. One would have to strive for a settlement that would enable the forces of Pathet Lao to rally and that would preserve the territorial autonomy and military independence of the Pathet Lao, even after the formation of a coalition government. Chen Yi concluded that the main enemy was the United States, and that no final solution would be possible as long as the United States maintained a military presence in Indochina. In line with this scenario, then, the Chinese delegation made preparations for a prolonged stay in Geneva.

Soviet impatience to arrive at a peaceful modus vivendi with the United States, aiming to reach a settlement in Laos as a contribution to obtaining détente in European and global affairs, evidently clashed with the Chinese resolve for a protracted military and political struggle against the US intervention in Indochina, a strategy rooted in national security concerns. The projection of divergent national security interests onto ideological obstinacy innately sharpened the controversies. Soviet-Chinese divergencies, as reflected in the above diverse scenarios, persisted and grew in the course of the Laotian crisis and the Second Indochina War. With national and security interests akin to Peking's anxieties, Hanoi leaned much more to the Chinese than to the Soviet position. In my encounters with North Vietnamese political and military leaders in Hanoi and their representatives in Laos, they particularly stressed the close interrelationship of the crisis in Laos with the developments in South Vietnam. They would agree to a political settlement in Laos only if this could open the way for a lasting political solution in South Vietnam as well.

In this, there was a parallel in political and military thinking with the policies of the United States. To the extent that the United States at times showed some interest in a political settlement in Laos, it was guided by the desire to demobilize and weaken the forces of the Pathet Lao and to cut the lines of communication between North and South Vietnam that ran through Laos. Laos itself was seen either in terms of a military-political steppingstone on the borders of Vietnam and China, or as a buffer intersecting infiltration routes between the two parts of the divided Vietnam. In the process, mutual stimulation between the essentially military-oriented policies of Hanoi and Washington served to aggravate the conflict. A ceasefire in Laos as envisioned by Pushkin and endeavoured by the ICSC was never formally concluded or fully observed in practice.

In this tangled situation I became locked between the diplomacies and strategies of East and West. What proved particularly difficult was to reconcile the disparate positions within the outwardly united "socialist camp". A kind of a balancing act was necessary here. On the one hand, I had to adhere to the basically conciliatory line followed by Moscow; indeed, I too sincerely desired a political settlement. On the other hand, I had to be attentive to the grievances of the Chinese. But mandatory to my behaviour had to be the policy of Hanoi and the Pathet Lao, the actual actors of the Left on the ground. I often voiced reservations to certain moves, preferring political rather than military pursuits, but ultimately I had to take into consideration the preferred general line of action of Hanoi and the Pathet Lao. The defence of the position of the Left was actually the unwritten role of the Polish delegation to the ICSC, as was the case for the Canadian delegation in relation to the right-wing forces. At times, I had to bow to the logic of war and violence as the only way to achieve preponderance in the given circumstances of a military conflict.

I was in regular contact with the Soviet and Chinese ambassadors, sometimes serving as in-between when they stopped talking to each other. This was a time without routine office work and protocol niceties. The air was full of gossip and almost daily revelations. The information and assessments gained from my camp-colleagues were useful and deepened my understanding of the nature of the conflict. But real insight and orientation on the course of events in the field could come only from the political and military leaders in Hanoi or their representatives in Laos and the leaders of Neo Lao Haksat. With them I developed close relations. It became clear to me that Hanoi was truly independent in determining its action, though paying lip-service to a common strategy. In certain sensitive issues pertaining to the Laos crisis and the Commission's work, Hanoi preferred to use me as a medium of communication to the Russians. Hanoi seemed disturbed by the divergencies between the Soviet Union and China. However, with time, it learned to exploit the competitive relations between Moscow and Peking to obtain more aid from one or the other ally, or from both together. Actually, in the long run, the Soviet-Sino clash was to help Hanoi to retain the relatively independent management of the conflict.

Looking back on my experience in Indochina, in the midst of the diplomatic-military mesh, I feel that I emerged richer in apprehension of the virtues and the wickedness of contemporary politics. The experience taught me to be averse to politics of the great powers and opposed to the use of violence, even in the pursuit of national liberation. I tried to perform the intricate balancing act between the diplomacies of East and West, and more so in the triangle of Moscow, Peking and Hanoi, to the best of my abilities, even though I sometimes felt uncomfortable in the jungle of great power and nationalist strife. For long periods, I had no instructions from Warsaw; I thus had some freedom of judgement and action. But halting the momentum of war was beyond the power of any outsider or the power of the ICSC. The experience of the ICSC has shown that control and supervision can be effective only when the parties themselves are interested in a ceasefire or a political settlement. Only when the parties – for whatever reason of their own, tactics and strategy included – chose to halt or to interrupt the fighting temporarily could the ICSC play a useful role. In the absence of goodwill from the parties, a control machinery could do little. I myself too often felt helpless and frustrated, faced with the fast-moving juggernaut of war.

2.5.7 Hanoi Vanquished

And later on, the epilogue was far from my liking. Given my solidarity with the struggle of the Vietnamese and Laotian peoples and hoping for an improvement in their lot at the end of the tunnel, I was deeply disappointed to see after the war that Vietnam and Laos remained among the poorest spots on the globe.

Not long after the US withdrawal from Vietnam, in 1978, I forwarded to the leadership in Hanoi a memorandum suggesting a radical shift from a military to an economic effort. What I had in mind was the need for an alternative development model that could enable a rapid rise in the standard of living of the population and perhaps even serve as a pattern for economic take-off for other Third World countries. My reasoning ran as follows: by defeating two major powers, France and the United States, Vietnam had shown unique feats of buoyancy, bravery and ingenuity. The time had now come to demonstrate a similar drive and inventiveness in the economic domain: to overcome underdevelopment and catch up with the advanced economies. From being in the forefront of the anti-colonial revolution, Vietnam should have moved to the forefront of economic development in the Third World. Developing nations were in dire need of a workable model of economic performance, which neither the East nor the West could provide. Given the Vietnamese independence of mind and action, Vietnam could show the way and start an entirely new experiment in development, in agriculture and industry, beyond systemic straitjackets, transcending the failures of the collectivist command economy of the Soviet Union and China. Obviously, such experimentation would require outside financial and technological support. My advice was not to accept conditional aid from great powers, East or West. It was vital to retain independence of action with leeway for experimentation. Instead, Vietnam should have solicited unconditional aid from smaller and neutral states, such as the Scandinavian countries or the Netherlands. In view of the sympathy Vietnam enjoyed, prospects for such support appeared good.

The initial response from Hanoi seemed positive. However, a follow-up, if indeed any was seriously contemplated, was not forthcoming. Hope seemed to evaporate and vanish in the blaze of the new conflict with Cambodia and China. Once again, the military option won the day. With more than a million soldiers under arms and heavy military expenditures, Vietnam's economy was deprived of resources and vision.

How did all this happen? A simplistic answer would maintain that generations of war and violence reproduced themselves in continued violence. A more commensurate explanation seems to lay deeper, anchored in the annals of history, geopolitics and surging nationalism. With France and the United States disappearing from the Indochinese scene, old local national contradictions came to the fore, unaffected by socialist professions. They became especially acute in the Vietnam-Cambodian-Chinese triangle, and the neo-colonialist contest channelled into a clash of indigenous nationalisms, intensified in the course of protracted warfare.

For all those who, pendent to the Indochina wars, had assumed the pre-eminence of international solidarity and lasting friendship between Vietnam, China and Cambodia, the chain of events that culminated in open warfare in early 1979 – with

Vietnam occupying Cambodia and China invading Vietnam "to teach a lesson" – must have come as a shock. But this reflected a historical continuity: nationalist antagonisms suspended and overshadowed by the Indochina wars came again to the fore. Socialism had done little to eradicate these trends. Though not fully noticed by foreign observers during the Indochina wars, national contradictions had persisted and even grown as resistance against foreign powers seemed to unite the Indochinese peoples. A key element in this process was the rise of the military potency of Vietnam. It brought a shift in the local relation of forces and prompted Vietnamese aspirations of dominance over all of Indochina.

The general background lies in the long annals of Chinese-Vietnamese conflictual relations, with China entertaining imperial ambitions to encompass the whole region into its sphere of influence. Throughout a thousand years of its early history, until the 10th century, the Vietnamese people had formed part of the Chinese empire; and for the next centuries, Vietnam was under constant pressure from China, suffering major Chinese invasions in the 13th and 15th century. Despite ages-long cultural assimilation, these conflict-ridden relations remained part of the historical memory of the Vietnamese. Again and again, I was struck by the depth of these feelings. Even when the bulk of aid to Vietnam during the Indochina conflict came from China, General Vo Nguyen Giap, the conqueror of Dien Bien Phu and Commander-in-Chief of the Vietnamese army, a former professor of history, reminded me of the past bloody chapters of the China-Vietnam history. The underlying understanding was that Chinese help, far from being altruistic, was motivated by utter self-interest. Vietnam's resistance against the foreign onslaught served as the first line of defence on the strategic "soft underbelly" of China.

Yet, following the US withdrawal, things changed radically. With Vietnam growing in resilience and military strength, the whole strategic constellation in the region became altered. Vietnam itself became a power centre with aspirations to rule over the whole of Indochina, Laos and Cambodia included. This turn to the South was again a historical regularity, as the conquest of the southern lands, including part of the Champa-Cambodian empire, was a feature of recent centuries only.

A little-noticed juncture in modern history came to play a crucial role in this respect. The mandate given to Ho Chi Minh by the Communist International (Comintern) in 1930 on the occasion of the establishment of the Communist Party covered the whole of the French colonial entity of Indochina. The party was baptized as the Indochinese Communist Party (ICP), though its founders were exclusively Vietnamese, with no participation of representatives from Laos or Cambodia. Invoking the spirit of internationalism, the Vietnamese direction of the ICP arrogated to itself the right to guide the revolution and the national movements, and consequently also to subordinate Laos and Cambodia to its leadership. Thus, the principle of Vietnamese domination was established. Imperceptibly, ideology came to uphold Vietnamese nationalist ambitions.

While I was serving in Indochina, this momentum became clear to me, although I could not realize the possible future consequences. Hanoi was always in command of the military operations and political undertakings in the whole of Indochina, including Laos and Cambodia. A special department at the Central Committee of the Vietnamese Workers' Party, headed initially by Nguyen Thanh Son and later by Nguyen Chinh Giao, acted as headquarters for the Left in Laos and Cambodia, and Vietnamese instructors and military units served as their backbone.

In the process, the dominance-dependence relationship and the sometimes heavy-handedness of the Vietnamese brought about disaccord in Indochinese Communist ranks. This ultimately channelled into an open conflict between Vietnam and the Khmer Rouge, the group was most distant from Hanoi and least amenable to control of the entire anti-American alliance. The Khmer Rouge combined radical nationalism with fanatical ideological paranoia. It recalled the glory of the Khmer Empire and became imbued by an originally French extreme doctrinaire revolutionary zeal. Facing Vietnam's expansionist pressures, Cambodia under the Khmer Rouge turned for help to China. Thus, the triangular conflict took shape.

In this nationalist involution lay perhaps the main roots of Vietnam's failure to reforge its military victory into an economic take-off. Relying on military power, Vietnam showed little flexibility to disentangle itself from the new regional conflict by pursuing a political solution as against the military option. Vietnam persisted in the occupation of Cambodia, while true national interests aiming at economic development required a historical compromise: peace as a precondition for an undisturbed devotion to the betterment of the human condition. This would implicitly necessitate a reconciliation with China and allowing Cambodia independence. Vietnam would have to give up the Comintern model of dominance over the whole of Indochina, replacing it with friendly relations with all its neighbours. By choosing a nationalist line compounded by military power, Vietnam lost a chance to emerge from the Indochina wars as not only the military victor but also as the architect of economic development.

The way the Indochina wars turned into a nationalist clash between countries that were once close allies was a hard blow to my expectations. Coming after my experience of "real socialism" in Poland, this brought added disillusionment about the true nature of statist socialism. It became evident that, similar to the Russian example, statist socialism also in the Asian countries was succumbing to traditional nationalist policies, sphere-of-influence designs and military power calculus. Events in Indochina, following the US withdrawal, reflected the dramatic global failure of statist socialism to uphold its professed ideals of human understanding and international solidarity.

Former allies have relapsed into enmity – a sad sequel to the Indochina wars. Will China, Vietnam and Cambodia manage to find the strength and wisdom to settle their differences peaceably and emerge as progressive states committed to lasting peace and a betterment of the human conditions of their peoples?

2.6   The Peace Research Chapter

2.6.1   Landing in Norway

Forced in 1968 to leave Poland, I found myself with my family in Norway, one of the birthplaces of post-World War II academic peace research.

I left Warsaw by train on the evening of November 29, 1968 and arrived in Oslo on the morning of December 1, 1968. My family joined me three weeks later via Vienna. My long journey led through the then Democratic Republic of Germany (Eastern Germany) and Sweden. The East German pass controller was somewhat startled examining my stateless Polish travel document: "What kind of identification paper is this? Are you a Polish citizen or not? Were you deprived of the Polish citizenship?" Anyhow, he was reassured noticing my entry visa to Norway.

In Oslo, I was met at the Central Railway Station by Tord Høivik, a senior researcher at the International Peace Research Institute, Oslo (PRIO), bearing a placard with my name. It was a warm welcome. The first thing Tord did was to hand over to me the key to the Institute. I was touched. Such a gesture of confidence would be unthinkable in the Eastern Europe of "real socialism", heeding to strict bureaucratic security rules. At the Institute, I was saluted cordially by the staff. An emotive note of welcome was posted on the information board. Everyone came to shake hands and to inquire about conditions in Poland. They seemed visibly gratified that PRIO could contribute to save a soul from persecution.

PRIO was at that time located in a spacious old patrician villa in the northern outskirts of the city, in a lovely surrounding near the great Holmenkollen ski jump and forested hills. I was accommodated in a large room and accorded living space for my family until such time as we were able to rent a flat. We were all overwhelmed by the amiable reception. We had the feeling of fugitives arriving at a gracious sanctuary. We were invited to the homes of PRIO associates and were shown around in Oslo and its beautiful environs. We were lucky to come into a milieu of committed young people, helpful and warm-hearted.

PRIO was then in its infancy. Founded in 1959 as a section of the Institute for Social Research, a private organization of social scientists, it was established as an independent institute in January 1966. The aura in the Institute was of idealism and optimism. Almost all the researchers, mostly young postgraduate students, had refused military service, substituting it through a time of duty as conscientious objectors. An expression of this defiant spirit was a pledge not to proceed with doctoral studies, which was meant as a protest against the university structure, thought to be of a feudal nature.

Members of the PRIO staff readily extended to me and my family a helping hand in all matters connected with the various problems of settling down in a new homeland. When I eventually rented a flat and worried about ways and means to move my belongings from the Warsaw packing crate, provisionally placed in the backyard of the Institute, to the new quarters, the PRIO colleagues spontaneously offered assistance. The Institute was closed for one day, one of the staff members provided a family transport lorry, and the whole staff worked as a team to carry furniture, books and household gear to my new domicile. The operation was carried out within the framework of *dugnad* – an old Norwegian custom of free neighbourly help. A true expression of inter-human friendliness.

Norway was a good haven for me and my family. An admirable country. Though, by chance, in Warsaw in 1967 I had edited an occasional paper on the historical background and development of the Scandinavian countries, my real knowledge about Norway was minimal. We were dazzled by its gorgeous nature: the fjords, the waterfalls, the mountains, the forests and the wide-open lands. And we were taken by the generosity of the people.

Materially, the beginnings were not easy. My initial stipend was not too high, barely sufficient to cover the family needs, and marshalling a new home required careful economizing. But, over time, we settled down well. My wife, Erna, liberated herself from the constant fear of ill winds in Poland. My elder daughter, Maya, finally found an attractive position as University Librarian at the University of Bergen. My younger daughter, Halina, after graduating in Polish linguistics at the University of Oslo, passed the examination as an authorized Polish-Norwegian translator, and landed as research consultant at Norway's Insurance Office. She married Johnny Lybæk, a Norwegian student of the Polish language, and gave birth to two sweet children, Petra and Susanna. And I myself found a gratifying engagement in peace research. The stay in Norway became one of the most productive chapters in my life.

2.6.2 The International Peace Research Institute, Oslo (PRIO) in Perspective

In the years after my arrival to Norway, the International Peace Research Institute, Oslo (PRIO) was in its youthful golden season. It was a time of elation, of theory-building in peace research and great expectations. The *spiritus movens* in peace research studies was the Director of the Institute, Johan Galtung. But ambitions to unfold and refine peace research were common to the academic staff. Discussions converged around the concepts of violence and non-violence, around conflict theory and conflict resolution, as well as compatibilities and incompatibilities of human values. Problems of war and peace were at the centre of attention. Peace was understood not only as the absence of war, but also as social justice, freedom, equity and satisfaction of basic human needs.

There was no precisely specified programme of studies imposed from above. Researchers were rather encouraged to work in fields of their own liking within the general framework of peace research. The Institute programme then consisted of the sum of studies by individual researchers. Individual thirst for knowledge and fervour were pivotal. In line with the egalitarian thinking, also the organizational structure of the Institute was not hierarchical. The Directorship rotated among all researchers.

I myself assumed the position of Research Director in 1979–1980, and then the duty as Director in 1981–82.

PRIO was, par excellence, an experimental institute. Theory-building in peace research was to go hand in hand with the Institute's internal life. The yearning for a just and equitable society found reflection in the Institute's remuneration system. In the beginning of the 1970s, the PRIO staff, about 20–30 people, together with conscientious objectors serving as research assistants, adopted a salary equalization scheme. It provided for equal salary rates for both the academic and the administrative staff, progression being dependent on work seniority only, with the duration of university studies counted as part of job seniority. There were thus cases where a secretary or a typist with longer working years would get a higher salary than a young researcher. The surplus payment in these cases would come from reduced researcher salary rates. The highest payment could not exceed the level of an assistant professor at the university. The theory behind this scheme idealistically assumed equal weight of research and administrative work. Moreover, it assumed that, over time, also members of the administrative staff would get involved in research activity.

The salary equalization scheme was worked out in great detail and an effort was made to get it approved by the authorities that provided the bulk of the Institute's budget. But eventually it did not stand the test of time. Some senior researchers left the Institute to accept better paid jobs at the University. Offering salaries below accepted rates in other scholarly institutions, it also became difficult to attract good researchers. Likewise, the assumption that the equalization scheme would stimulate greater research enthusiasm, involving the administrative staff as well, did not materialize. In the mid-1980s, the equalization scheme was abandoned.

Was this a sign of PRIO's coming of age and settling down as an established institution, with all the inherent managerial structures? Or was it one of the symptoms of the decline of idealism and the acquiescence to power structures in human and international relations? Actually, in 1987, PRIO adopted a bureaucratic and hierarchical line-up, with the Director concentrating much of the executive authority and peremptory rule, and the well-selected Board serving in the main as his rubber stamp. A rather common practice. This went hand in hand with the thinning out of peace research in the direction of establishment-oriented strategic studies, to suit the agenda of the authorities handing out the funds for the maintenance of the Institute. It was about this time in 1989, coinciding with my retirement age, that I was obliged to leave PRIO and moved to the Norwegian Institute of Human Rights.

2.6.3 Evolution in Peace Research

There was some parallelism with the general evolution of post–World War II academic peace research sliding progressively in its mainstream to programmes and activity near the seats of power. As a new scholarly discipline, peace research was born within the social sciences in the 1950s and 1960s as a conscientious revulsion against the Cold War and the danger of human annihilation by nuclear weapons.

It was Albert Einstein who first came forward with the memorable warning that "the unleashed power of the atom has changed everything, except our way of thinking". Peace research took up the call for a new way of thinking in questions of war and peace. Its original aim was to critically study the causes of war and the conditions for peace. Ideally, this required a multidisciplinary paradigmatic effort in such fields as history, economics, political science, sociology and international law, as well as, increasingly, hard sciences and technology critical for the emergence of modern weaponry. It was thus no coincidence that the founding fathers of modern peace research were prominent scholars from different disciplines: the economist Kenneth E. Boulding (USA), the sociologist Johan Galtung (Norway), the game theorist Anatol Rapoport (Canada), the international lawyer Bert V. A. Röling (the Netherlands) and the political scientist David Singer (USA).

Stimulated by the newness of this discipline and its value-orientation, peace research experienced a tangible expansion in the 1970s. Substantially, its very conceptualization has been deepened. Constantly redefining and widening the concept of peace, it advanced from simple notions of the absence of war and manifest physical violence, termed negative peace, to the positive, victim-oriented definition of peace encompassing social justice, participatory democracy, civic freedoms, respect for human rights and ecological balance. Methodologically, both normative theory and empiricism came to guide peace research studies. In the process, peace research established itself as a distinct value-loaded and applied discipline aimed at radical transformation of society and international relations with the maximization of peace in its positive conceptualization as its central value.

Immediately, there arose tension between the ideal socio-political vision of peace research and its application. What ways and means would be required to carry into effect social justice, abolition of oppression and the affirmation of civil liberties? Would this call for violent, revolutionary methods? The general response of peace research was a preference for non-violent action. Studies have been initiated in non-violent civilian defence, civil disobedience and "people's power" confrontation in the struggle for political and systemic change. Developments on the verge of the 1980s and 1990s in Eastern Europe and the former Soviet Union seemed to vindicate the pertinence of non-violent strategies for change.

Even so, peace research had no ambition to become a political movement. Its self-image was of a scholarly undertaking, with the findings perceived as an educational input into the struggle for progressive change. It had to contribute to delegitimize and stigmatize power politics, militarism, oppression, authoritarian rule and violation of human rights. It aimed to indicate alternative ways of peaceful and humane governance.

In its evolution, peace research established some general priorities in its studies. Three fields of attention were predominant: (a) the Cold War armaments and problems of disarmament, (b) underdevelopment and maldevelopment in the Third World, and strategies of change, and (c) freedoms and respect versus violation of human rights. These three clusters were seen as interrelated. Human and material resources wasted for excessive armaments deprive humanity of assets urgently needed for development. At the same time, underdevelopment and the disparities between developed and developing countries, apart from being a sore human issue, contribute to international tension and conflict. And suppression of freedoms serves to feed militarism, authoritarian rule and unrest. The three currents meet in breeding violence.

The general critical orientation of peace research was not very much to the liking of established authorities. From its beginning, peace research faced a problem of funding. A particular example of financial strains encountered by peace research was the systematic reduction and finally the complete withdrawal of official support in Germany, one of the countries with a rather wide network of peace research. Thus, in the course of passing the 1992 federal budget, the Household Commission of the German Lower House (*Bundestag*) decreased the support of peace and conflict research by one million Deutschmark (from 2.85 to 1.85 million). Independently, the Federal Government had already decided during its intermediate budget planning sessions to reduce the remaining funds until 1994 and cut them entirely starting in 1995.

It soon transpired that with sparce resources, in-depth studies requiring both inter-disciplinarity and broad area-studies was beyond the reach of peace research. In the process, peace research became marginalized within social studies. Cold War pressures added to enfeeble its effort. On the one hand, East and West perspectives met to entangle peace research in strategic studies, with the 'realistic' balance of power paradigm seen as peace-promoting. On the other hand, this contributed to inner polarization, with affected extremism winning ground. Thus, peace research was losing much of its initial originality and independence of thought. While largely accommodating to the political agenda of the ruling establishment, the critique concentrated more on ways and means of the political-military drive than on visionary alternatives. Counting weapons and their employment obscured the need for a fundamental peaceful reordering of human and world affairs. Superb individual scholarly achievements were unable to make good of the falling reputation of peace research.

After three decades of expansion, its impetus stagnated. The number of peace research institutes around the world adhering to a positive definition of peace remained small, perhaps not surpassing a two-digit number. Their scholarly staff counted mostly only a few researchers. They were mainly located in the Nordic countries, in Western Europe and in North America. Peace research in the Third World, with the exception of India, was hardly visible. There existed also some university departments of conflict and peace research scattered around the globe with a scant number of scholars attached. Some individual social scientists occasionally identified themselves as peace researchers. A specific case was institutes of international relations in the 'socialist' countries fully subjected to government control, which for political reasons joined the peace research movement. The meeting point for peace research of different orientations was the International Peace Research Association (IPRA), founded in 1965. At the 25th Conference of IPRA in Groningen (the Netherlands) in 1990 there were, according to the official account, 361 participants from 57 countries, including non-scholarly peace movement activists and representatives from international bodies. IPRA had an affiliation of 816 individual and 136 corporate members covering 71 countries, with the academic record of its members being very uneven. The renowned Stockholm International Peace Research Institute (SIPRI) has not joined IPRA.

The atmosphere of crisis in peace research deepened with the collapse of the communist regimes in Eastern Europe. A considerable share of peace researchers had socialist leanings. They tended to look on the evils in the East with less doom than the predicaments in the West. The prostration of "real socialism" was a source of confusion. Studies stimulated by an eagerness to bridge the gulf between the East and the West, based on the assumption of power symmetry, lost their meaning. Many of the dreamed-of models of equivalent European security faded away. A considerable portion of peace research, in parallel to the peace movements, found it difficult to absorb and digest the unexpected and volatile developments.

All this brought about unruliness in the ranks of peace researchers. Was it only a transient crisis or a sign of a more lasting quiescence? In the meantime, the plurality of what remained of peace research concentrated on a manifold of subjects, such as problems of ecology, internal conflict, conversion of military potentials, peace education, refugee problems, feminist attitudes, national concerns and related issues. Would this help to restore the relevance of peace research in national and international conflictual situations, as an explicit academic discipline concerned with studies on the causes of war and conditions for peace?

Nevertheless, I recall the over 20 years of my peace research vocation with much delight. It enriched my scholarly pilgrimage and offered out-of-the-ordinary opportunities to meet similar-minded, concerned people and formations around the world, West and East, North and South. I cherished particular contacts with scholars and scientists of high standing, with a long-life experience in political and military affairs, such as Nobel Prize laureates and pragmatists who attended the birth of the atomic age. Listening to them added to my insight into the ups and downs in peace and war of the 20th century.

2.6.4   The Bulletin of Peace Proposals (BPP)

In 1968, I was invited to PRIO to launch a new quarterly peace research journal devoted to peace schemes and conflict resolution. The new periodical was meant to be published in parallel to the *Journal of Peace Research*, established in 1964 and edited by Johan Galtung. The title suggested by Galtung for the new journal was *Bulletin of Peace Proposals* (*BPP*). My initial concept was to collect and abstract official documents and records of various international bodies and actors, as well as papers and statements of individual scholars and politicians relevant to conflict resolution and peace-making. These would then be classified and discussed in the light of peace research theory so as to advance the pursuit of peaceful solutions to current conflict situations. Subject to these compilations would be problems of the Cold War, of armaments and disarmament, underdevelopment and development, of ongoing conflict such as Vietnam and the Middle East, of the violation and affirmation of human rights, of the role of science and technology in peace and war, and, last but not least, peace research theory in its relevance to conflict resolution.

In 1969, I edited two Xeroxed trial issues of the *BPP*, in spring and autumn, as well as a volume of documents on *Vietnam Peace Proposals, 1954–1968*. As from 1970, the *BPP* appeared in printed form as a regular quarterly published by the Norwegian University Press (Universitetsforlaget). The journal had a fairly good reception, particularly in peace research and international studies quarters, though paid subscriptions (at a rather high price) rarely exceeded 900 copies. Currency difficulties impeded wider circulation of the journal in the East and South. I had to make up for this deficiency by sending out a number of copies free of charge.

Until my retirement from PRIO, up to the end of 1988, I edited 76 issues of the *BPP*, i.e. 19 annual volumes, some of them containing up to 600 pages. As from mid-1970, I modified the profile of the journal. Instead of featuring peace proposal abstracts, I concentrated on analytical papers from scholarly and political quarters addressing central and acute contemporary problems of peace and war, of conflict and conflict resolution. Six special issues of the journal (No. 1/1979, No. 1/1983, No. 3-4/1986, No. 3/1987, No. 4/1987 and No. 1/1988) were re-edited and published in cooperation with other scholarly institutions as topical books.[xiv]

Editing and publishing the *BPP* was a source of great satisfaction. It felt good to be on the ethical-moral side of the eternal human exertion for progressive change. Far beyond the paid subscriptions, the journal reached a relatively large readership of concerned students of international relations and politicians aspiring for a value-based gauge in international and inter-group affairs. Young students perused the journal at university libraries and used them in their courses. The *BPP* became standard reading and a point of reference for a number of intellectuals and professionals interested in equitable solutions for ongoing conflicts. The feedback was encouraging. Critical voices concerned mainly the spectrum of the journal, the inclusion or non-inclusion of specific items pertaining to conflict situations and peace making.

But editing the journal and assuring its regular appearance required much work. PRIO had very limited resources and I was left almost without editorial assistance as well as without secretarial and administrative help. I had to plan and commission papers and edit the materials. One of the handicaps was that we had no means to pay fees to the authors. At the same time, I had to engage in fundraising to cover the high publication costs, which exceeded the incomes from subscriptions. I was then overloaded both with editorial and executive work. Nearly a one-man show. I often complained to the PRIO leadership and at staff meetings. In response, there was only appreciation for the work done, yet no change in the routine.

All the same, it was a rewarding job. For one thing, it served as a stimulus to deepen the understanding, philosophy and assumptions of peace research. Adding to my previous professional and life experience, I felt I was gaining a more comprehensive, sound and soft world view. I had no illusions that there are shortcuts for global peaceful transformation, aiming at a decent, civilized and non-violent world. But it was challenging to be part of efforts in this direction. Actually, the self-conception of peace research was less of political activism and more of a scholarly spurt to guide the political process on a course consonant with basic human values.

I was then tempted to share my thoughts, reflections and research findings with the readers of the *BPP* and beyond. Thus, I engaged in writing on current issues of peace studies and international relations. My list of publications has grown steadily. Moreover, through the *BPP* and as a Senior Research Fellow of PRIO, I established contacts and became involved in the activities of a number of international scholarly institutions and organizations concerned with problems of peace and war and the betterment of the human condition. Meeting scholars and politicians from different countries and quarters, and critically testing diverse approaches and judgements on ongoing peace-relevant affairs, in theory and practice, served as food for thought. I was frequently invited to various international scholarly meetings and conferences in Europe (West and East), Asia, the United States, Canada and Latin America, contributing papers and acting as resource person. The *BPP* editorial work, doing research, writing and active participation in international communication and deliberations on problems of war-avoiding and peace-making filled the chapter of my engagement in peace research.

Still, looking back on my involvement in peace research, I am not particularly content. For one thing, peace research in its institutional and substantial evolution fell short of its initial aspirations. Its impact on world affairs was minimal. Both in the domain of armaments and disarmament and of reordering of international relations, the powerful and wealthy continued to dominate the flow of events. In my contacts with international government and non-governmental organizations, including the different United Nations bodies, I had often a distinct feeling of confronting an impasse system, full of lofty words but short in resolute meaningful deeds. The general outcome was of swimming with the tides of the hegemonial powers. Those within this game would always say that politics is the art of the possible. This may to some extent be true. Change is a long-term generational undertaking. Yet I was impatient for radical departures in our times. Maybe I initially put too much faith in the validity of peace research and the susceptibility of expedite reform of the international system. Evidently, I underestimated the tenacity and perseverance of the conflict and war structures. Though a student of history, I failed to reconcile with its intractable power-political course.

2.6.5   On Being Part of the Peace Research Community

I came to peace research with much enthusiasm. I saw in it a kind of continuation and pursuance of my youthful ideals of a just and equitable world. In my research and writings, I followed the mainstream of peace research priorities. Apart from the *BPP* and the six books which I edited as a follow-up of the *BPP*, I also edited four topical books on armaments, militarism and nuclear disengagement in cooperation with UNESCO, the Stockholm Peace Research Institute, the Pugwash Conferences on World Affairs, the Commission on International Affairs of the World Council of Churches and the International Peace Research Association (IPRA).[xv]

On top of these books, I published three books of my own on the war in Indochina, military technology and the post–Cold War armaments momentum.[xvi] My list of publications from 1968 to 1991 includes, too, over 130 papers and articles devoted to topics ranging from armaments, disarmament, arms control, and the related working of military research and development (R&D); to the interrelationship between disarmament and development; to international conflict situations such as the war in Indochina; to militarism and militarization; and, last but not least, to problems of peace research, its theory and practice. A considerable number of these papers deal with questions of the Cold War arms race and its dynamics, as well as with its temperance and cessation. In this context I attached particular importance to the role of modern science and technology and its R&D drive, both as a stimulant to armaments and as a potential material force for reordering world affairs, aiming at the betterment of the human condition.

Historically, the focus on the working of science and technology proved to be opportune. The revolutionary rise of science-based modern technology in the post–World War II period was of supreme significance for the course of contemporary national and international affairs. From a macro-historical perspective, as seen at the close of the 20th century, no single occurrence did more to change the face of the world then the explosion of science-founded high technology, civilian and military. Its impact pervaded all spheres of human life: social, economic, political and cultural. In many ways, the play of modern science and technology revealed its double-edged nature, with a potential for good and evil. It became the backbone and anvil of a new economic take-off and of a new race in armaments. The problem before humanity was and is to shift priorities and bring about a limitation and conversion of the military exertion, especially of military R&D, for peaceful purposes.

Driven by modern science and technology, armaments got a new impulsion. They moved in the main from a race in quantities to a race in military technology. Inhibitions inherent in high costs and the saturation of arsenals became muted by the sustained competition in ever new-born military technology. This actuated a propensity to reach out in the arms build-up far into the future, to get ahead of the adversary. Thus, armaments became more complex, costly and enduring. The arms race acquired an unprecedented ferocity and became a global phenomenon. Even with the end of the Cold War, technologically-impelled armaments persisted. Nuclear weapons remained suspended like a Damocles sword over humanity and ever more sophisticated conventional weapons continued to be developed in the military workhouses.

The impact of the buoyant ascension of modern science and technology went far beyond the armaments dynamics. Commanding the most advanced technology and R&D potentials became crucial for wealth and power. Monopolization of R&D capability by the developed countries contributed to deepening the disparities between the rich North and the poor South.[xvii] Moreover, the imbalance in the acquisition of modern science and technology between the East and the West played an essential role in shifting the relations of force between the developed West and the 'socialist' East, leading finally to the demise of the Soviet empire.[xviii] The spread and growth of computer sciences, electronics and robotics gave birth in the West to the information and consumer society, largely absent in the Soviet empire. On the one hand, communist systemic secrecy was inimical to informatics. On the other hand, Cold War strategies isolated the East from the scientific-technological advances in the West. Whatever new technology was available was monopolized by the military, leaving the civilian sector in ever greater decay. Consequently, the uneven pace of development amplified the industrial-technological gap between West and East. The Soviet Union increasingly hung back in developmental capability, lagging behind the West even in the military domain. In conjunction with the systemic deficiencies and the burden of armaments, it finally lost the very staying power of the empire and collapsed.

The rise of modern science and technology, with its subsequent societal impulses, affected even the sphere of the ideological superstructure in the Soviet Union. Marx's ideas had originally been shaped by the initial stages of the Industrial Revolution and the rise of imperialism. At that time, the oppressed low-paid labour force formed the main industrial phalanx: hence the focus on the class struggle. But the scientific-technological revolution of the mid-20th century has brought about a radical shift in productive forces as well in the structure of society. The underpaid proletariat has largely been replaced by the middle classes: computer scientists, technicians, engineers, teachers, physicians. The emergence of the information and consumer society in the West, with rising standards of living, encouraged dissidence in the East. Dominant class-based orthodox ideologies lost flesh and pressures for change proliferated. Even not fully perceiving the depth and speed of the socio-economic and political global avalanche prompted by the revolutionary flare-up of modern science and technology, I was from the beginning of my involvement in peace research intellectually attracted by studies on the role and impact of modern science and technology on society. Their exertion through massive investments in R&D became one of the central topics in my research and writing.

Part of my main concern was to promote action for change: how to restrain military technology, make modern science and technology work exclusively for the good of mankind, and empower the scientific community as a material force for human progress. In a paper presented at the 22nd Pugwash Conference on Science and World Affairs, held in Oxford in September 1972, I dealt with the social responsibility of scientists and tried to outline proposals for how to activate the scientific community, aiming for "a world more human, more rational, more just". I wrote:

Scientific inquiry, research and development have come to occupy a pivotal position in shaping the fate of mankind ... Yet in few fields of scientific inquiry are the social consequences of new discoveries and technologies thoroughly studied and clearly anticipated ... While the scientists and engineers form the creative nucleus behind the development of modern science and technology, they are practically deprived of any power to decide on the use made of their toil. The power generally rests with the managerial bureaucratic elite which dominates state and private interests ... In this context, because of the complexity of modern science and technology, because of the place new discoveries occupy in contemporary society, because of the uncertainties linked to the use made of these inventions and because of the far-reaching implications they may have – the social responsibility of the scientist becomes historically more crucial than ever before. No scientist can possibly abdicate the responsibility for his work and the use made of it. Every scientist has a right and duty to demand participation in considering the eventual application of his discoveries and toil … Moral judgement is needed to make knowledge more human and wiser … The key issue is to steer the up till now loosely understood responsibility of scientists and engineers to concrete socio-political action … The primary objective of the scientist's action would have to be directed towards openness of research and use of modern technology. Two problems seem central to this effort: a free, considered debate on research and development within the scientific community, and a regular dialogue with society, reporting to the general public and popularising the essence of new departures in science as well as their possible social implications.[xix]

In concrete terms I suggested:

> … to raise social awareness and professional ethics by introducing an oath for scientists and engineers similar to the Hippocratic Oath of the medical professions. The wording could contain both a negative and positive pledge: not to use the scientific training for any purpose which may harm human beings; and to devote the acquired knowledge to foster human progress, the betterment of life, freedom, justice, and peace.

Moreover, I proposed:

> …to enact a procedure in research and development by which a certain percentage of funds earmarked for technical projects should be habitually devoted to simultaneous research on the social consequences of the project and its application … The above proposal … may be linked to a requirement for setting up a development fund financed by a fixed percentage of resources devoted to armaments …

Of political importance would be a concrete project to regularly channel concerned information from the scientific community to the general public, so as to draw national and international attention to critical issues of modern science and development, and open research problems to public debate and consideration.[xx]

2.6.6   The Case of Establishing an International Disarmament Fund for Development

Few, if any, of the proposals for progressive change forwarded by the concerned scholarly community and by me in Oxford were assimilated in action on the international scene. Suggestions like the introduction of a Hippocratic Oath for scientists and engineers or the establishment of an independent Technological Assessment Authority were repeatedly voiced in gatherings of conscientious scientists. Yet they did not meet the approval, or even the attention, of established powers. They were left in abeyance, as a kind of eternal apprehensive qualm of the troubled scholarly community.

However, over time, one idea attracted greater international interest: the institutional linkage between disarmament and development, and the establishment of an

International Disarmament Fund for Development (IDFD). This idea even came near to fruition, to be eventually wrecked by great power resistance. I invested much effort to make the project work and felt frustrated at its final repudiation.

The history of the aborted attempt is worth telling.

For a long time in the United Nations debates, an intimate relationship has been perceived between efforts at slowing down and halting the arms race, and the real-location of funds released by disarmament for economic and social development, particularly to eradicate the poverty in the Third World. With finite resources available to the international community for global economic growth and sustained human development, it seemed natural to cover the deficiencies through cuts in the excessive spending on armaments. In different versions and forms, the idea sporadically surfaced as a remedy to ease the predicaments of armaments and underdevelopment. However, more often than not, suggestions to the above effect forwarded by different countries, among them the Soviet Union and France, had a rather rhetorical ring, aimed to serve diplomatic and political craft. At best, they were presented in visionary terms, far from prospects of practical implementation.

A new occasion for taking up the question of establishing an IDFD arose at the close of the 1970s, following the rather sterile UN Disarmament and Development Decade. On the initiative of the Nordic countries – Denmark, Finland, Norway and Sweden – the UN General Assembly Special Session on Disarmament decided to commission an expert study on the relationship between disarmament and development. It was natural that such a study should examine, among other things, the propriety and convenience of founding an IDFD. The Group of Governmental Experts set up by the UN Secretary-General for the elaboration of the study commissioned a number of preparatory research reports. I was invited to produce one such report on establishing an IDFD.

I submitted my research report in summer 1980. Its policy recommendations concluded i.a.:

> The time seems ripe for action. The world needs some practical expression of the benefits which can accrue by linking disarmament and development ... The ideal future model for contributions to the Fund should be seen as based on resources released as result of disarmament and arms control measures such as global, regional and bilateral agreements. This model should be adopted as a statutory aspiration of the Fund. In line with this, one should aim to establish through UN action the basic requirement and rule that future disarmament and arms control agreements should: (a) clearly indicate and spell out the financial savings resulting from these agreements; (b) state the way the dividends would be calculated, i.e. the economy in human and material resources; and (c) provide for the allocation, possible through the Fund, of resources saved, either for conversion purposes or development goals ...[xxi]

I presented detailed proposals as to the various contributions to the fund and suggested to assign to the fund in the initial stage between 0.5 and 1% of annual global military expenditures, as a minimum. This would at that time amount to about one billion US dollars annually.

The UN Study *The Relationship Between Disarmament and Development*, published in 1982, advocated the establishment of an IDFD.[xxii] It pointed to the political desirability of such a fund and discussed the principles for its founding as well its operational vulnerabilities, delineating guidelines for further considerations of its working structures. In December 1982, the UN General Assembly mandated the Geneva-based UN Institute for Disarmament Research (UNIDIR) to undertake additional studies concerning the working structures of the fund. I was again one of the researchers invited to participate in this project. In March 1984, I submitted my complementary study, "Modalities for the Establishment of an International Disarmament Fund for Development: Vision and Political Feasibility".[xxiii]

I dealt in the study with the conceptual assumptions of an IDFD relating to disarmament, development, and their interrelationship, as well as their import for peace and security, and suggested optimal solutions for establishing the fund:

First and foremost is the prerequisite of voluntary consensual action of the United Nations family of nations. Willing endorsement of the scheme is essential for its success ... The Fund should be able to generate a long-term political process which can effectively act to link disarmament and development functionally. Finally, an essential principle to be aspired is universal participation ... To avoid hurdles stemming from tangled controversies related to measurement, comparability and verification of military expenditures, the key solution lies in adopting the principle of voluntary contributions based on the widely recognized general orders of magnitude of military spending. The respective concrete shares would then be left to negotiations between the interested parties ... As for the problem of disbursement ... it would be proper that up to 50% of the resources released by the disarmament (budgetary) measures should be earmarked for development in the donor countries. One particular purpose should specifically be kept in mind and accorded high priority: conversion of parts of the military industry into socially useful civilian production aimed to satisfy unmet needs of the society ... Specific attention should be given to the conversion of military research and development into civilian research and development, the prime mover of modern economy ... Concerning the question of disbursement of development aid to Third World countries ... a basic dual criterion for development aid would have to be applied: it should be geared to the promotion of both disarmament and development ... Parallel to this, development guidelines should preferably be oriented towards stimulating self-reliance; development aid should provide resources, in addition to autonomous national efforts, to eradicate poverty and furnish the productive strata of the population with basic human needs as well as tools for the advancement of the economy ...[xxiv]

In its concluding report to the United Nations, UNIDIR took a most positive stand concerning the establishment of an IDFD.[xxv] It was almost taken for granted that such an IDFD would see the light of day.

Yet the UNIDIR report had a mixed reception. While acclaimed by a majority of the UN member states, it received a cool welcome by the major powers who were not particularly eager to see any institutionalization of the linkage between disarmament and development and not willing to be pressed on both issues. Consequently, the UN General Assembly adopted a resolution to again temporize with the whole issue. The December 1984 resolution 39/60 expressed the need "to review the relationship between disarmament and development in all its aspects and dimensions" and "consider ways and means of releasing additional resources, through disarmament measures, for development purposes, in particular in favour of developing countries".

Years passed, with behind-the-scenes negotiations on further action. Eventually, after arduous preparations, an International Conference on the Relationship between Disarmament and Development (ICRDD) was convened in New York under the aegis of the United Nations, from August 24 to September 11, 1987.

It proved to be a disappointing exercise. A total of 150 UN member states took part in the conference, with the notable exception of the United States. The USA dissented with the very idea of the conference, arguing that disarmament and development are distinct processes and should be pursued separately, regardless of the pace of progress in each of them. In this basic stand the USA had the support of its major allies. Under their pressure, the idea of establishing an IDFD was removed from the agenda of the ICRDD even in the preparatory stage of the conference. No mention of it was made in its Final Document, which confined itself to some high-sounding general statements on the need of attitudinal change in problems of armaments-disarmament and underdevelopment-development on moral, ethical, political and economic grounds. But there was no sign in the Action Programme of how to proceed with real deeds, how to make disarmament work or how to promote development.[xxvi]

I myself tried in the corridors of the ICRDD to highlight the importance of establishing an IDFD. Through the Conference Secretariat, I circulated two Non-Governmental Organization documents: (a) remarks on the "Draft for a Final Document of the ICRDD", and (b) a paper entitled "The Quest for an International Disarmament Fund for Development: Linking Peace and Security with Associative Development Efforts".[xxvii]

In my remarks on the Draft for the Final Document of the ICRDD, I took exception to its frame of reference, and particularly "the lack of concrete measures to operationalize in political-economic terms the relationship between disarmament and development". In the 'Quest' paper, I discussed the philosophy behind the idea of an IDFD, its political acceptability, and operational feasibility, and concluded:

Not only would setting up of an IDFD operationalize disarmament and development imperatives, and open alternative vistas for security: such action would also generate perceptional and attitudinal shifts of political and educational import. By its very novelty and new perspective, the Fund can affect the general climate of international relations, promoting such basic values as peace, common security, human understanding, mutual respect and a sense of togetherness of the global family of nations ... It would tend to de-emphasize enemy images and introduce a learning process on the nature of common interests. It would motivate lower reliance of force in international relations, promoting instead reason, rationality and realism in seeking peace and human fulfilment through the assurance of basic human needs for all ...[xxviii]

Alas, appeals for the establishment of an IDFD went by like a call in the wilderness.[xxix] The power structures within the United Nations prevailed, compounded by bureaucratic inertia. As the Secretary-General of the ICRDD, Jan Mårtenson, remarked: in pursuit of a consensus at the Conference, including the stand of the major powers, "we have to cruise between Scylla and Charybdis: between coming out with platitudes and watered-down statements and asking for too much".[xxx]

Eventually, indeed, platitudes and watered-down statements were to win the day. The idea of establishing an IDFD was discarded. I was upset by the abortion of the project. Beyond the resentment about the dismal performance of the United Nations, I took it almost as a personal defeat.

2.6.7   Military Research & Development – The "Holy Fire" of Armaments

The failure of the project to establish an International Disarmament Fund for Development is but one example of the eternal contention against greater political-structural odds which are the fate of numerous concerned efforts at progressive change. Nevertheless, these are not completely lost battles. They leave behind an educational effect which becomes part of the slow historical transformation of society. New thinking and alternative action require time to mature. They may also require a propitious political climate and favourable international fortune to materialize.

Another domain, perhaps even more essential, to which I attached particular attention, and where I tried, without success, to develop a research project for change was military research & development (R&D). This was related to my general interest in the role of science and technology in contemporary society. My studies, conducted on the background of growing Cold War armaments, led me to findings which pointed to the crucial role of military R&D in the arms race. The huge military R&D establishment, employing hundreds of thousands of the best qualified scientists and engineers globally, nurtured particularly by the major powers, became the breeding ground and engine of armaments.

There was then a need to make this exertion transparent, to learn more about its modes of operation, in order to restrain its drive and, possibly, to bring about its conversion for peaceful purposes. Again, in this case, a research project initiated within the United Nations was aborted, and my personal endeavours to establish a research project with the participation of concerned scientists and scholars also did not come to fruition.

Early in 1975, I drafted a manifesto of the Disarmament Study Group of IPRA, *Between Peace and War: The Quest for Disarmament*, in which I said:

Three decades after World War II, man is again armed to the teeth with armaments reaching levels unequalled in history … The arms race is in both conventional and nuclear weapons, in quantities and qualities, horizontally and vertically … Armaments continue unabated, parallel and despite détente … The world cannot possibly continue in this aberrant way if it cares about the fate of mankind and, above all, if it wants to tackle effectively and solve the presently critical problems of poverty, hunger, pollution and diminution of resources … At present, the dominant feature in conventional and nuclear weaponry is constant modernization and innovation of the weapon systems ... A ghost-like, self-perpetuating driving force behind armaments is to be found in the extensive military research and development (R&D) – the actual core and forge of qualitative weapon advancement ... No disarmament strategy can possibly succeed without taking into account the crucial role of military R&D in the arms race, without trying to find ways and means to bring it under control and eventually convert it to peaceful purposes ... Of overriding importance for all activities aiming at disarmament is the limitation of as much as possible of the atmosphere of secrecy surrounding armaments, and the pressing for greater openness in information, debate and negotiations. Secrecy in armaments contributes not only to overreaction, and to the fostering of armaments dynamics, but also adds to a general malfunction of society in many domains ... Openness means democratization of the very disarmament process, broader knowledge and greater participation of public opinion. By making things transparent, openness could prove to be the most effective weapon against all vested interests in the armaments establishment ...[xxxi]

Fully grasping the intricacies and hazards of the technological momentum in armaments dynamics, I pursued my research on the working of military R&D. In the scholarly debates on the relative import of the external action-reaction inducements to armaments versus the internal socio-economic and technological motive forces, I tended to attach greater importance to the internal factors. They seemed to me of much deeper and long-term duration, even beyond the Cold War, embedded in structural peculiarities of the post–World War II new military-industrial power impulsions. In these inner-fuelled dynamics I saw military R&D as a primary agent, with R&D visualizing the research process as an endless continuum, and the technological imperative imparting on this process a momentum always to reach out to the frontiers of new-won technology. In a paper published in 1981 in *Impact of Science on Society*, I tried to indicate the perceptible mode of operation of military R&D which perpetuates armaments:

No single sphere of human activity exerts a greater impact on contemporary society than military research and development (R&D). Military research does this in two ways: on the one hand, by serving both as a pace-setter and accelerator of the arms race, and, on the other hand, by perverting values and distorting priorities in science ... The huge proportion of resources appropriated to military R&D leaves little funds for research focused on bettering the human condition ... The skewed distribution of resources and their quantitative computations, however, do not tell the whole story. More important is the qualitative aspect, the institutional set-up and mode of operation of military R&D ... Five major structural factors can be distinguished in the dynamics involved.

First, the impact of the competitive drive within the mammoth empire of military R&D. This adds vitality and serves as an energizer of the arms race on the one hand, and acts to assert the dominant influence of military R&D in civil branches of the research enterprise, on the other hand ...

Second, ... the long lead-times required to develop new weapon systems and introducing them unto the armamentarium ... assure constancy and continuity within the armaments process ...

Third, the so-called follow-on imperative and growth propensity of military R&D … feeds the arms race … Expansion is part of the very nature of military R&D …

Fourth, much of the strength and innovative capability of military R&D lie in the block-building and cross-fertilizing effect by which projects, initially unrelated but complementary in their technologies, meet to accomplish breakthroughs and produce entirely new weapon systems …

Fifth, structurally related to the rising power of military science is the mighty socio-political constituency of military R&D …

Thus, military R&D cannot be apprehended and analysed in static terms. It is one of the most dynamic institutions of our time, acting with resolution and aggressiveness … Yet military R&D is related not only to questions of peace and war. It also has to do with a general malfunction of society … Basic human values such as peace, security, freedom of research and speaking out against its misuse, and the right to democratic participation in shaping research – all these are at stake … We need more research, action-oriented research, to make military R&D more transparent, to help to change priorities in all R&D, to further disarmament efforts and introduce an element of social control in the activities of military R&D.[xxxii]

I returned again and again to the theme of the role of military technology in the arms race, as well as a detrimental factor in the human scientific endeavour. In February 1982 I presented my views at the joint UNESCO-Pugwash Symposium in Ajaccio (Corsica), devoted to "Scientists, the Arms Race and Disarmament". In my paper on military R&D, I noted.

One of the main characteristics of the contemporary arms race is the science-based fixation on an intensive technological thrust … New weapon systems tend generally to act as catalysts for new political and strategic departures. They actually arrogate to themselves a political function … Politics tends to lose its autonomy, yielding ever more to the dictates of technology … The transformation of the scientific pursuit in the military domain into a mammoth technological effort rigorously institutionalized in the military R&D establishment has enormous consequences for society … Penetrating almost all disciplines of hard and soft sciences, it assumes a commanding position in global research and development arrogating a strong influence on the direction of the scientific endeavour not only in the military but also in the civilian domain …[xxxiii]

In 1982 I took part in a scientific symposium organized by the Nordic Academies of Sciences and Letters devoted to ethics in scientific research. In my paper dealing with values and ethics in the scientific endeavour as related to military R&D, I remarked:

On a very general level, the problem concerns the location of military R&D on the axis of the positive and constructive versus the harmful effects on society. Given the double-edged nature of contemporary science, military R&D almost by definition serves to sharpen the edge of injury and destruction. Ideological justifications on patriotic-nationalistic grounds – actually stronger in the East than in the West – do not rock on the fundamental realities of the scientific undertaking and its application … In addition, the structural framework and regimentation in military R&D are fundamentally antithetical to the norms, standards, and ethics of true science. There is a contradiction between the ethics of science and the regulations/restrictions that military R&D imposes. In military R&D there is no openness, little autonomy, scant right to publish freely and to speak out, and highly restricted freedom of inquiry. These are not minor violations of professional ethics in science. Instead of entertaining channels of communications to the academic community and society at large, to assess in common the consequences of inquiry and collectively make rational choices, military R&D acts in secrecy. It stimulates fragmentation of the scientific community … Instead of maintaining and developing standards of academic and intellectual integrity, and of true civic responsibility, military R&D tends to pervert human values about the sanctity of life; it obscures basic moral dilemmas in relation to peace and war, and suppresses feelings of social and moral responsibility …

Concerning the dilemmas facing scientists who serve military R&D, the issues boil down to the question of compatibility in a triangle whose sides are the ethical principles of national security, of scientific professional ethics and values, and broad human-social ethical values with special reference to human life/needs and total/annihilation warfare. It must rest with the conscience of the individual scientist to draw the proper conclusions. No scientist can divorce himself from the use made of his discoveries, nor avoid bearing a heavy social and moral responsibility for his engagement.[xxxiv]

The problem of the qualitative arms race fuelled by military R&D became increasingly a source of international concern. The First Special Session of the UN General Assembly Devoted to Disarmament, convened in 1978, stated in its Final Declaration:

Mankind today is confronted with an unprecedented threat of self-extinction arising from the massive and competitive accumulation of the most destructive weapons ever produced … Qualitative and quantitative disarmament measures are both important for halting the arms race. Efforts to that end must include negotiations on the limitation and cessation of the qualitative improvement of armaments, especially weapons of mass destruction and the development of new means of warfare so that ultimately scientific and technological achievements may be used solely for peaceful purposes.[xxxv]

As a follow-up to the First Special Session of the UN General Assembly on Disarmament, the General Assembly on December 16, 1978, decided to initiate a *Comprehensive Study on Nuclear Weapons*. The study was completed in 1980 and its conclusions amounted to a severe indictment of the qualitative arms race:

It is clear that in many cases technology dictates policy instead of serving it, and that new weapons systems frequently emerge not because of any military or security requirement but because of the sheer momentum of the technological process.[xxxvi]

The Second Special UN General Assembly on Disarmament convened in 1982, at a time of the resurgence of the Cold War, was less outspoken and could only note that "there has been no significant progress in the field of arms limitations and disarmament, and the seriousness of the situation has increased."[xxxvii] Still, encouraged by the quality and broad appreciation of the *Comprehensive Study of Nuclear Weapons*, the 1982 regular UN Generally Assembly passed a resolution

...to carry out a comprehensive study on the scope, role and direction of the military use of research and development, the mechanisms involved, its role in the overall arms race, in particular in the nuclear arms race, and its impact on arms limitation and disarmament, particularly in relation to major weapon systems, such as nuclear weapons and other weapons of mass destruction, with a view to preventing a qualitative arms race and to ensuring that scientific and technological achievements may ultimately be used solely for peaceful purposes.[xxxviii]

From the start it became transparent that such a study would encounter difficulties from the major powers addicted to military R&D. The first indication came with the setting up of the group of governmental experts that had to produce the study. Previously, at the time of commissioning the *Comprehensive Study of Nuclear Weapons*, the nuclear powers declined to participate in the drafting body. But, learning a lesson from this study, which was not to their liking, this time the nuclear powers joined the group of governmental experts to prepare the new study. The purpose could well be envisioned: the study should not interfere with the exertion of military R&D.

In accordance with the usual UN practice, the *Comprehensive Study on the Scope, Role and Direction of the Military Use of Research and Development* should have been produced in a year's time and presented to the UN General Assembly in 1984. Yet because of divergent views within the expert group, the deadline had to be twice extended until 1986. Still, even though the study was watered down to the extreme, there was no unanimity in its final wording. The major nuclear powers retained some basic objections.[xxxix]

Faced with this situation, the 1986 UN General Assembly by a vast majority voted for the publication of the study, with indications where consensus could not have been achieved. However, ultimately this procedure was discarded. To suit the attitude of the major powers, which did not favour any insight into military R&D, the UN Secretary-General finally decided not to publish the controversial text of the study.

This was the only case in the history of the United Nations that a study commissioned by the General Assembly did not appear in print. A stranded effort.

I myself, taking advantage of my book *Military Technology, Military Strategy and the Arms Race* published in 1986, tried to draw attention to the aborted study of the United Nations and activate the concerned scientific community as well as international bodies dealing with problems of armaments and disarmament to undertake in-depth studies on ways to restrain military technology. I turned to the Pugwash Conferences on Science and World Affairs, to SIPRI, the UN University, UNIDIR, the UN Department for Disarmament Affairs and others. Of no avail.

At the 36th Pugwash Conference in Budapest in September 1986, I presented a paper in Working Group 1 entitled "Restraining Military Technology Crucial for Arms Control and Disarmament".[xl] In its report, Working Group 1 then noted:

... one of the main driving forces behind the arms race is the unchecked momentum of modern military technology. Thus, effective arms control and disarmament require that this technological momentum be curbed. It was suggested that Pugwash establish a study group on ways to restrain military technology.

I followed this postulate up at the 37th Pugwash Conference in Gmunden (Austria). But the Pugwash Council did not take action. It is possible that the reason lay in a lack of resources to organize a broad study. But it is also possible that the Pugwash Council, dominated by American and Russian scientists, perceived in such a study a minefield which would be difficult to cross.

In the meantime, I approached American scholars with a similar request. At the Budapest Pugwash Conference, we tentatively agreed to convene a planning meeting in the United States. Prof. Franklin A. Long of Cornell University undertook to initiate preparative steps with the American Academy of Arts and Scientists.

In parallel, with the promulgation of *glasnost* and *perestroika* in the Soviet Union, I contacted the Committee of Soviet Scientists for Peace and suggested a workshop on ways of restraining military technology, to be convened in Moscow in spring 1987. I held talks in Moscow on this subject in February 1987, invited by the Soviet Academy of Sciences to attend the Forum of Scientists on the Reduction of Nuclear Weapons. I presented at this forum a paper on "The Quest for Restraining Military Technology".[xli] The forum, the first large Gorbachev manifestation of new thinking in foreign policy (with the attendance in our group of academician Andrei D. Sakharov, just returned from his exile in Gorky), provided an opportunity to initiate discussions on a possible joint project in the domain of military R&D.

I returned to Moscow in May 1987, invited to serve as moderator in a panel on "Comprehensive Test Ban Agreements: History and Prospects" at the Seventh World Congress of the International Physicians for the Prevention of Nuclear War. In my panel I presented a paper entitled "The Pursuit of a Comprehensive Nuclear Test Ban: Curbing the Arms Race and Checking the Quest for Exotic Weapons".[xlii] But I used the occasion to continue discussions on a research project devoted to military technology.

I was received by the Deputy Director of the Institute of the USA and Canada of the USSR Academy of Sciences, Dr. Andrei A. Kokoshin (later Minister of Defence of Russia in the Yeltsin government), with the attendance at our discussions of Dr. Mikhail I. Gerasov, a Senior Research Fellow at the Institute. In our exchange of views, we agreed on the paramountcy of military R&D in the qualitative arms race and on the need to devise strategies for checking the technological armaments momentum. I then pleaded for greater openness of Soviet military R&D so as to complement the insight from Western sources and be in a position to better face the task of curbing military technology. I indicated that there seemed to be a willingness of American scientists to participate in a joint US-Soviet research project on the above subject. Kokoshin showed interest in the scheme. But concerning Soviet participation or independent initiatives, he felt that the Soviet military would not yet be willing to open up in such a critical domain as military R&D. Time was needed, he said, to mellow this stand. He suggested that I should try first to arrive at concrete results in the United States, and then, possibly, the Soviet scientific community would follow. I was not happy with this hesitation. But it seemed to reflect Soviet realities with a sincere willingness to overcome the structural obstacles posed by the military-industrial complex.

I had then to intensify my efforts in the United States. I agreed with Prof. F. A. Long to convene at the American Academy of Arts and Science (AAAS) at Cambridge, Mass. A planning workshop on qualitative criteria for arms control and disarmament in August 1987, coinciding with my attendance in New York at the International Conference on the Relationship Between Disarmament and Development. I suggested an agenda which would include three main points: (a) Nature and Role of Military R&D, (b) Intricacies of Restraining Military Technology, and (c) Action Programme. The last point would concentrate on initiating an expert transparency study on the military use of R&D, to fill the void left by the abortive UN study; establishing a study group on ways to restrain military technology; and establishing an international Standing Assessment & Reporting body on development in military technology, possible under the auspices of the Pugwash Conferences.

The planning workshop met at the AAAS at Cambridge on August 20, 1987. Among the participants, apart from Professor F. A. Long, were Professors Harvey Brooks and Ash Carter from Harvard, Professors Carl Kaysen and Kosta Tsipis of MIT, Randall Forsberg from the Institute of Defense and Disarmament at Boston, Professor Judith Reppy from Cornell, as well as Jeffrey Boutwell and Joel Osten from AAAS. We had an intense daylong discussion which touched on a wide range of problems, from questions of data and the intricacies of the working of military R&D, to the increased militarization of R&D in the wake of the Strategic Defense Initiative. Concerning the identification of new research projects, two trends emerged.

I suggested the establishment of a Study Group on the introduction of qualitative restraint into arms control and disarmament efforts. However, a majority of the participants seemed more concerned with the predicaments of US military R&D (waste, low efficiency) and its negative impact on the US economy (high military and low civilian funding of R&D). In questions of restraining military R&D, they advocated to retain a (moderate) hedge against the technological advances of the Soviet Union. To preserve the technological advances in the arms race was of primary concern, a kind of a technological imperative.

With this 'patriotic' functional state of mind of the US scientists active in military R&D, prospects of a joint US-Soviet research project to constrain military technology, beyond the established arms control exercise of joint balanced steering of the arms race, looked dim. In these circumstances I could not possibly have expected the Soviets to be willing to give up their technological hedge against the West. It seemed futile to turn again to Kokoshin.

In the meantime, even with the end of the Cold War, military technology impelled additionally by the tests of the Gulf War remained a key element in unremitting armaments. Characteristically, in all the main arms control agreements, from the 1972 Strategic Arms Limitations Talks (SALT), through the 1987 Intermediate-range Nuclear Force accord (INF), up to the 1990 Conventional Armed Forces Reduction in Europe (CFE), and the 1991 Strategic Arms Reduction Talks (START), one provision continued to be constant: modernization and innovation of weapons and weapons systems were not even mentioned. Military R&D would still be permitted. Indeed, it has remained the "sacred cow" and "holy fire" of armaments. The battle against the pivotal military component of the war engine was definitely lost. Military R&D is to persevere far into the 21st century.

2.7   Aiming at a "Culture of Peace" Based on Human Rights

2.7.1   A Time of Reflection

After the retirement from PRIO, I had been fortunate to find a niche for further research and study at the Norwegian Institute of Human Rights (NIHR). A helping hand in this passage was extended to me by Asbjørn Eide, the Director of NIHR, a former senior researcher at PRIO with whom I shared a number of publication projects.

In its research, NIHR concentrated mainly on the universal legal aspects of the human rights project, with reference to case studies as to the observance or violation of the human rights law. This gave me the opportunity to get a deeper insight into the international instruments of the human rights project, their potency and weaknesses.

My specific interest related to the essentials, the historical background, the philosophical prerequisites as well as the existential substance of human rights in daily life and international relations. I perceived the human rights project as a viable tool to bring about progressive change in human affairs, nationally and internationally.

The human rights project was close to my concerns. Its appeal consisted in an interface with positive peace as envisaged in peace research theory. However, with my life experience and the memory of my unfulfilled dreams, I embraced the human rights project with gentle moderation. More and more I came to comprehend progressive change as a non-linear, prolonged process. NIHR was a good haven for reflection – past, present and future.

I became particularly attached to a project launched by UNESCO on the concept of "culture of peace", which, I felt, could best be articulated within the framework of the human rights project. It offered fitting universal rules and moral-ethical norms, open and dynamic, to guide human behaviour so as to establish a global culture of peace. I came to assume that no international charter or political-philosophical tenets can mirror the spirit of a culture of peace and serve its purpose better than the legal foundations of human rights. The human rights project may ideally serve as a functional infrastructure for a culture of peace.

In co-operation with NIHR, UNESCO and the Nobel Peace Committee, I edited an anthology on peace, as perceived by the Nobel Peace Laureates during the 20th century, between 1902 and 1992.[xliii]

The volume contains a set of abridged versions of the Nobel lectures and/or acceptance speeches by the Nobel Peace Prize Laureates, as well as by those delivering lectures on behalf of organizations that have been awarded the Nobel Peace Prize. My guiding principle of the selections was to retain all elements relevant from the substantial, historical, legal, political and analytic-scholarly point of view.

To make the message of the Laureates more lucid and transparent, I classified the material into seven thematic chapters: (1) The meaning of peace; (2) The instruments for peace policies; (3) The peace movement and the pacifist world-view; (4) Armaments and disarmament; (5) Human rights, welfare and social justice; (6) Humanitarian challenges; and (7) Regional conflicts. Thus, the anthology in a way reflects the thorny efforts at peace-making in the 20th century – the course of events, the general reasoning of Nobel Peace Laureates and the struggle to develop both principles and institutions to serve the cause of peace.

The anthology makes instructive reading. With all the merits of the individual and collective non-governmental laureates at peace-making – in forging instruments for peace policies, in humanitarian efforts, in paving the way for non-violent solutions of conflicts, in struggling for disarmament – a narrative evolves of an up-hill, Sisyphean struggle to civilize human relations.

The 20th century has been marked by persistent 'peacelessness', by a void of freedom from want and fear, by ceaseless armaments, enduring arms races and intermittent wars, hot and cold, by the rise of weapons of mass destruction, by the killing fields of genocide and Holocaust. True, there were also moments of hope, as after World War I and World War II, with the establishment of the League of Nations and the United Nations, which promised to free the world from the scourge of war and stirred hopes for the establishment of positive peace.

Yet little has been achieved in this respect. Even after the Cold War, instead of the heralded benign New World Order, humanity was troubled by insecurity, conflict, regional wars, "ethnic cleansing", hundreds of millions of hungry people in the South and a sense of turbulent disorder. The promised peace dividend vanished. A generic, sombre feature of the international scene in the 20th century has been an almost exclusive discourse in terms of power politics and power relations. Horizons were overcast by a state of mind presuming in effect an innate alienation and enmity between nations and societies, between the mighty and the weak, between the have and the have-nots – a momentous deficit in moral-ethical deportment.

2.7.2   Challenges Before the Human Rights Project

Rooted in the Enlightenment and modernization of recent centuries, the human rights project emerged after World War II as a revulsion against the barbarity of war, as a beacon of light for the humanization of national and international relations. Its main yearnings and ideas were inscribed in the International Bill of Rights, consisting of the 1948 Universal Declaration of Human Rights (UDHR) and the 1966 two International Covenants on Economic, Social and Cultural Rights (CESCR), as well as on Civil and Political Rights (CCPR).

In the process of expansion of the human rights code, the International Bill has been complemented and spelled out in greater detail by a number of United Nations conventions, declarations and recommendations, covering such basic domains as the Right to Self-determination; Prevention of Racial Discrimination; Rights of

Persons Belonging to National, Ethnic, Religious and Linguistic Minorities; Rights of Women; Rights of the Child; Human Rights in the Administration of Justice; the Right of Freedom of Information; the Rights to Social Welfare; Humanitarian Law etc.[xliv] Of particular importance, though less followed up, are the rights concerning socio-economic and political solidarity, the Right to Development and the Right of the Peoples to Peace. They are crucial for the generation of a substantial and veritable culture of peace.

Furthermore, the international human rights instruments were complemented by regional instruments of the Council of Europe, the Organization of the American States, the Organization of African Unity and the Organization of Security and Co-operation in Europe. Special mention should be made of the European *Social Charter* of the Council of Europe, which seeks to secure ingredients of the welfare state.[xlv]

Potentially the provisions of the human rights project are intended to cover all aspects of life in dignity, freedom, security and peace. As such, the human rights project is highly demanding. It is value-loaded and future-oriented. Though not all of the instruments of the human rights project are juridically binding, they are norm-setting for a virtuous and civilized global culture of peace.

Effective implementation of the human rights instruments is proceeding slowly. Some are still rather of a visionary – aspirational and promotional – nature, and vague in the articulation of normative and legal implications. Comprehensive observance of all human rights provisions – according to their letter and spirit – is rare. Their violation is frequent in all corners of the globe. Also, many provisions inscribed in the human rights instruments lack tangible substantial formulations and are often vague and diffuse. This is particularly true of economic, social and cultural rights. On the other hand, the provisions for civil and political rights are often used as a point of contention against the less developed countries. A basic deficiency of most of the instruments is the lack of mechanisms providing for complaints by victims of violation of rights and for appropriate redress. In addition, many human rights provisions are not inscribed in state legislations. A number of Third World countries even question the universality of the human rights project, assailing it as 'Western' and "Euro-centric", with limited attention for Asian/Eastern values and the needs of developing countries. Some governments did not subscribe to many instruments of the project, while others temporize with the ratification of accepted instruments.

Thus, the full implementation of the human rights project would seem to prognosticate a protracted process. Its progression poses an immense challenge for the establishment of a genuine, non-violent culture of peace.

In two papers on "The Philosophical-Existential Issues of the Human Rights Project: Challenges for the 21st Century", and "Towards a Culture of Peace Based on Human Rights", I tried to elaborate on the predicaments of the human rights project which impede the constitution of a culture of peace.[xlvi]

Seen in the context of dominant policies and strategies of the great powers and a majority of states, characterized by the so-called *Realpolitik*, the very concept of a culture of peace appears illusory if not utopian. Contemporary *Realpolitik* at the seats of power is in fact socio-politically permeated by an impulse to violence and war. It treats peace in an expedient, instrumental way, with war – in the classical Clausewitzian mode – envisaged as a continuation of peace by other means and methods. Such orientation gives rise to a state of mind which professes the virtue of armaments and soldiering, as well as all sorts of military deterrence, i.e. constant preparation for war, as a prudent implementation of security postures, with no cognition that throughout history arms races have in fact generated conflict and war. Moreover, such an amorphous 'culture', intertwined with global socio-economic stratification and pauperization of large parts of the international community, begets human estrangement, hatred and enmity between peoples and nations – a destructive penchant to pathologies of domination, ethnocentrism and xenophobia.

The materialization of the human rights project requires thus a vigorous, wide-open and expansive agenda:

First is the pursuit of a mature constitutional democracy in line with the human rights provisions. Actually, there is a close affinity between the well understood human rights code and democracy. Observance of human rights is the litmus test of democracy. Likewise, genuine democracy must strive to enact and implement the provisions inscribed in the human rights instruments. This refers above all to the observance of civil, political, economic, social and cultural rights as inscribed in the two International Covenants on Civil and Political Rights as well as Economic, Social and Cultural Rights – with particular emphasis on the rule of law and regard to the four basic freedoms: freedom from want and fear as well as freedom of speech and belief. Inherent in these rights is the individual right to life, liberty and security. In human rights theory, civil and political rights on the one hand, and economic, social and cultural rights on the other hand are closely interrelated, indivisible and interdependent. A basic precondition for the success of such a viable democratic society is an educational effort to lift the consciousness of the people so as to repudiate power relations based on violence and strive instead for tolerance, willingness to compromise, mutual understanding and common security required for the pursuit of a culture of peace.

Second, in close relation to the vision of a universal culture of peace comes the emphasis on social development, social justice and human advancement on a global scale. The positive conception of peace perceives an organic linkage between intranational and international violence, and seeks parallelly to eliminate the seeds of peacelessness, both internally and externally. In this respect there is a generic connection between the provisions of the International Covenant on Economic, Social and Cultural Rights and the 1986 Declaration on the Right to Development.[xlvii] The Declaration on the Right to Development perceives development as a "comprehensive, economic, social and cultural process, which aims at the constant improvement of the well-being of the entire population and of all individuals on the basis of their active, free and meaningful participation in development and their fair distribution of benefits resulting therefrom". Thus, both a national and an international effort is required. As a solidarity right, the Declaration emphasizes that "as a complement to the efforts of developing countries, effective international co-operation is essential in providing those countries with appropriate means and facilities to foster their comprehensive development". Although the Right to Development has no legally binding force, its message – with a view to reducing poverty in developing countries and eliminating conflictual relations on the North-South fault line – is compelling.

Third, as a critical case in national and international relations, special attention has to be given to the elimination of virulent ethno-nationalism, xenophobia and political-religious fundamentalism pregnant with terrorism and endangering peace in many parts of the world. The entire human rights project must be harnessed for this effort.

Fourth, the pursuit of a culture of peace requires the recognition of pluralism within and between societies. We must be attentive to the diversity of civilizational/cultural world-views and behaviours – ethnic, national and religious – within the family of nations. Cultural diversity is a historical reality of our world. Acknowledging these circumstances, the Universal Declaration of Human Rights provides for freedom of opinion and expression, and for free participation in the cultural life. To this effect, the Universal Declaration calls on every individual and every organ of society to "strive by teaching and education to promote respect for these rights and freedoms … to secure their universal and effective observance".

Fifth, last but not least, is the fundamental task to preserve and promote international peace. There is an urgent need to operationalize and infuse life into the Right of Peoples to Peace, as inscribed in the human rights project.

2.7.3   The Right of Peoples to Peace

The Right to Peace is endorsed in two instruments of the human rights project: the 1984 UN General Assembly Declaration on the Right of Peoples to Peace[xlviii] and the 1986 UN General Assembly Declaration on the Right to Development.

While non-binding, these two solidarity rights are of supreme importance. Aiming at a substantial completion of the human rights project so as to generate a solid infrastructure for a culture of peace, the Right of Peoples to Peace needs to be elevated to a legally mandatory status, with precise provisions in content and executive clauses, in procedures and enacting mechanisms, nationally and internationally.

In its Preamble, the Declaration on the Right of Peoples to Peace emphasizes "the will and the aspiration of all peoples to eradicate war from the life of mankind and, above all, to avert a world-wide nuclear catastrophe". Further, that "in the nuclear age the establishment of a lasting peace on Earth represents the primary condition for the preservation of human civilization and the survival of mankind".

In Article 1, the Declaration "solemnly proclaims that the peoples of the planet have a sacred right to peace", and stresses in Article 2 "that the preservation of the right of peoples to peace and the promotion of its implementation constitute a fundamental obligation of each State".

The Declaration, then, in Article 3, "emphasizes that ensuring the exercise of the right of peoples to peace demands that the policies of States be directed towards the elimination of the threat of war, the renunciation of the use of force in international relations and the settlement of international disputes by peaceful means on the basis of the Charter of the United Nations".

Finally, in Article 4, the Declaration "appeals to all States and international organizations to do their utmost to assist in implementing the right of peoples to peace through the adoption of appropriate measures at both the national and international level".

Some provisions for the consummation of the Right of Peoples to Peace are spelled out in the Declaration on the Right to Development. This Declaration points first of all to the interrelationship between disarmament and development. In its Preamble, the Declaration reaffirms "that there is a close relationship between disarmament and development and that progress in the field of disarmament would considerably promote progress in the field of development".

Most notable is Article 7, which states: "All States should promote the establishment, maintenance and strengthening of international peace and security and, to that end, should do their utmost to achieve general and complete disarmament under effective international control, as well as ensure that the resources released by effective disarmament measures are used for comprehensive development, in particular that of the developing countries".

Intimately linked to the Right of Peoples to Peace is the "inherent right to life" as inscribed in Article 6 of the International Covenant on Civil and Political Rights. Commenting on the right to life, the Human Rights Committee, mandated to critically consider the observation of the International Covenant on Civil and Political Rights, noted:

It is a right which should not be interpreted narrowly ... The Committee observes that war and other acts of mass violence continue to be a scourge of humanity and take the lives of thousands of innocent human beings every year ... The Committee considers that States have the supreme duty to prevent wars, acts of genocide and other acts of mass violation causing arbitrary loss of life. Every effort they make to avert the danger of war, especially thermo-nuclear war, and to strengthen international peace and security would constitute the most important condition and guarantee of the right to life.[xlix]

This reflects supreme concern about the fate of mankind. Bearing in mind this conclusion, the Human Rights Committee draws particular attention to the perils of the stockpiling and further development of nuclear weapons, which could lead to nuclear catastrophe.

We all need to be reminded in this context of the hazards of nuclear proliferation as exhibited in spring 1998 by the acquisition of nuclear weapons by India and Pakistan. With the end of the Cold War, our general awareness of the global vulnerability from the stockpiling and development of nuclear weapons and other weapons of mass destruction has diminished. Yet the doomsday legacy of the nuclear arms race, the stockpiling of nuclear weapons and their modernization are still with us.[l] Thus, in the military mind, nuclear weapons are still perceived as useful and required for defence-offence purposes, under the name of legitimate nuclear deterrence.[li]

As long as the major powers see nuclear weapons as necessary and useful for defence and war, weaker states will strive to follow suit and acquire nuclear capability as a shield against stronger neighbours or pressures from great powers. Actually, continued stockpiling of nuclear weapons by the major powers is a recipe for nuclear proliferation.

Here we should also note that the nuclear danger is only the most conspicuous element of current armaments. Despite the end of the Cold War, the production and trade in conventional weapons has not ceased. Cut-throat competition has developed between the major powers and weapon producers to deliver these arms to almost all corners of the world.[lii]

As never before, the solidarity Right of Peoples to Peace, calling for the elimination of nuclear weapons, General and Complete Disarmament and demilitarization of international relations has acquired an importance which is critical for a transition from a war system to a peace system, from military to political solutions in human affairs.

In recognition of this emergency, the Nobel Peace Committee awarded the 1995 Nobel Peace Prize jointly to Prof. Joseph Rotblat, the President of the Pugwash Conferences on Science and World Affairs, and to the Pugwash Conferences on Science and World Affairs for their long-time struggle for disarmament and the abolition of nuclear weapons.[liii]

Denuclearization, the implementation of General and Complete Disarmament and demilitarization of international relations remain the supreme goals for the operationalization of the solidarity Right of Peoples to Peace.[liv] They are essential for a functional global human rights regime designed to generate a universal culture of peace. The Right of Peoples to Peace is morally legitimate and needs to be empowered with legal authority. It has to be anchored in the international legal order – with a substantive content and definitive mechanisms – so as to assure freedom from fear, nationally and internationally, and to become a material force in pursuit of a culture of peace.

2.8   Epilogue: Plus Ça Change, Plus C'est La Même Chose

I would very much like to conclude the reflections on my journey through the 20th century in a positive, hopeful mood. After all, great, beneficial socio-political and economic-technological changes took place in the past century, such as the abolition of slavery; the elimination of colonialism; the rise of the human rights project; some advances in welfare; a curtailment in gender inequalities; the revolution in almost all sciences, hard and soft, from the explosion of information technology to the expansion of transport and the progression in medical sciences, physics, chemistry, and microelectronics; and finally the spread of democratic ideas and greater openness in national and international affairs.

The advances are unquestionable. However, the deep structures of 'peacelessness' in military and socio-economic affairs prevailed. Lack of freedom from want and fear remain potent. The world is still dominated by old-style divisive politics, by ethno-nationalist and religious conflicts, by armaments, militarization of international relations and deep cleavages of a socio-economic and political nature.

2.8.1 The Military Laboratories

First come military affairs. According to the Stockholm International Peace Research Institute's *SIPRI Yearbook 1998*, the best currently available estimate of world military expenditures suggests that the total amount of money devoted to military activities amounted to around $740 billion in 1997.[lv] Relying on several other reliable sources, the UN *Human Development Report 1998* states that world military expenditure in 1997 reached $780 billion[lvi] – a sum which could redress all shortcomings in global human development. The interesting thing with the *Human Development Report 1998* is that it lists at the same time annual expenditures on items of "the world priorities". Thus, on basic education for all, the world spends only $6 billion; on cosmetics in the USA $8 billion; on water and sanitation for all $9 billion; on ice cream in Europe $11 billion; on reproductive health for all women $12 billion; on perfumes in Europe and the USA $12 billion; on basic health and nutrition $13 billion; on pet foods in Europe and the USA $17 billion; on cigarettes in Europe $50 billion; on alcoholic drinks in Europe $105 billion; on narcotic drugs in the world $400 billion. There is something incomprehensible in these figures.[lvii] A record of a skewed socio-civilizational conduct.

Armed conflicts in 1997 continued unabated. Major armed conflicts – defined as prolonged combat between the military forces of two or more governments, or of one government and at least one organized armed group, incurring the battle-related deaths of at least 1000 people during the entire conflict and in which the incompatibility concerns government and/or territory – were waged in 1997 in 25 instances and in 24 locations throughout the world. All but one of the conflicts in 1997 – that between India and Pakistan, focused on the Kashmir issue – were internal.[lviii]

Civilian fatalities have climbed from 5% of war-related deaths at the turn of the century to more than 90% in the wars of the 1990s.[10] Recent times have witnessed new weapons and patterns of conflict, including the indiscriminate use of land mines and antipersonnel cluster bombs, as well as a proliferation of light weapons. As a result, many of the casualties are women and children. Over the past decade, armed conflicts have killed 2 million children, disabled 4–5 million, and left 12 million homeless.[lix]

With reference to part 6.7 on the role of military research and development (R&D), the most mischievous aspect of contemporary armaments consists in the long-term consequences caused by the constant development of entirely new sophisticated and

---

[10] This figure is now disputed. Cf. Adam Roberts (2010) 'Lives and statistics. Are 90% of war victims civilians?' *Survival* 52(3): 115–136. (The editors.)

lethal weapons – such as directed and kinetic energy weapons, including lasers, neutral and charged particle beams and radio frequency beams, all with precision guidance and very high velocities with space-basing options – to be employed in all theatres of future wars. The push effect in this domain lies with the exertion of military R&D, particularly by the major powers. Global expenditure on military R&D in 1996 amounted to $58 billion, of which the NATO countries spent $48 billion. The United States alone invested $37 billion in military R&D in 1996, a level similar to that in 1983 – the year in which the United States launched its ominous Strategic Defense Initiative.[lx] At the same time, the Russian government funding for military R&D has fallen dramatically from the levels sustained by the Soviet Union during the Cold War – having reached a level perhaps of 90% lower in real terms.[lxi] Moreover, official figures may not reflect the full extent of expenditures on military R&D as today more R&D is funded privately, with close ties to military R&D.

A particular feature of current military R&D – as noted in the *SIPRI Yearbook 1998* – is that "new technologies are developed but not necessarily built and deployed".[lxii] This follows the pattern as envisaged in 1990 by two prominent scientists of the Los Alamos National Laboratory, Joseph F. Pilat and Paul C. White, who argued: "If one believes that the world is poised on the threshold of a military-technological revolution, and that the prospect of East-West conflict in the next ten years is low, than greater emphasis should be placed on R&D and modernization than on maintaining current active force levels. Traditional Western reliance on technology will grow, not diminish in the years ahead ... Prudence dictates a shift in emphasis from deployed to deployable forces, entailing an R&D program designed to provide a range of rapidly producible and deployable weapon systems".[lxiii]

The above policy is in line with the steep rise of military technology during the 20th century, from the First and Second World Wars through all the military testing fields in Korea, Vietnam and the Gulf war. Current military R&D seems to get the world ready for disastrous surprises in warfare of unpredictable consequences.

Besides, international tension is bound to be exacerbated by the shift from a bipolar to a multi-polar world. In the process, the axes of conflict tend to multiply and become inflamed by nationalist-civilizational and religious-fundamentalist fault-lines.

2.8.2   The World Socio-Economic Balance Sheet

As we approach the turn of the century, with a deep crisis engulfing the emerging markets in developing countries, the fallible socio-economic balance-sheet of capitalist globalization becomes apparent.

Globalization was heralded after the Cold War as an era of growth, welfare and global human advancement. The reality belies the prophets of market-financial expansion. The *Human Development Report 1998*, focusing on consumption, health, knowledge and a decent standard of living, both in developing and developed countries, outlines a rather sombre image of the working of globalization. With consumption as the main criterion, the report states:

The 20th century's growth in consumption, unprecedented in its scale and diversity, has been badly distributed, leaving a backlog of shortfalls and gaping inequalities.[lxiv]

Furthermore:

Globalization is integrating consumer markets around the globe and opening opportunities. But it is also creating new inequalities and new challenges for protecting consumer rights.[lxv]

The poorer 20% of the world's people and more have been left out of the consumption explosion. Well over a billion people are deprived of basic consumption needs. Of the 4.4 billion people in developing countries, nearly three-fifths lack basic sanitation. Almost a third have no access to clean water. A quarter do not have adequate housing. A fifth have no access to modern health services. A fifth of children do not attend school to Grade 5. About a fifth do not have enough dietary energy and protein. Micro-nutrient deficiencies are even more widespread. World-wide, 2 billion people are anaemic, including 55 million in industrial countries. In developing countries, only a privileged minority has motorized transport, telecommunication and modern energy. Inequalities in consumption are stark. Globally, the 20% of the world's people in the highest-income countries account for 86% of total private consumption expenditures – the poorest 20% account for a miniscule 1.3%."[lxvi]

Essentially, globalization aimed to force open new markets around the world, especially in developing countries, for the expansion of products and financial capital of the mighty companies and entrepreneurs, enhanced by powerful advertisement and information technology. The global advertising spending, by the most conservative reckoning, is now $435 billion annually.[lxvii] Globalization generated an economic global power elite and a global middle-profiteering-class propelling the ventures of the big and mighty. The global order generated by globalization is dominated by the rich and vigorous, while the weak and the poor are marginalized and excluded.

The gross inequalities between the rich and the poor did not shun the industrial countries. Studies of poverty in the developing countries – with low levels of resources and human development – focus on hunger, epidemics, illiteracy and lack of health and safe water. These issues are less dominant in industrial countries. But studies of poverty and deprivation in the more affluent countries concentrate on social exclusion. The *Human Development Report 1998* notes.

On the basis of an income poverty line of 50% of the median personal disposable income, more than 100 million people are income-poor in OECD countries; at least 37 million people are without jobs in OECD countries … ; unemployment among youth (age 15–24) has reached staggering heights, with 32% of young women and 22% of young men in France unemployed, 39% and 30% in Italy and 49% and 36% in Spain; … Nearly 200 million people are not expected to survive to age 60; more than 100 million are homeless, a shockingly high number amid the affluence.[lxviii]

To illustrate the momentous global inequalities, a special box in the *Human Development Report 1998* is devoted to "the ultra-rich". It states:

New estimates show that the world's 225 richest people have a combined wealth of over $1 trillion, equal to the annual income of the poorest 47% of the world's people (2.5 billion) … The three richest people have assets that exceed the combined

GDP of the 48 least developed countries ... The assets of the 84 richest people exceed the GDP of China, the most populous country, with 1.2 billion inhabitants ... It is estimated that the additional cost of achieving and maintaining universal access to basic education for all, basic health care for all, reproductive health care for all women, adequate food for all and safe water and sanitation for all is roughly $40 billion a year. This is less than 4% of the combined wealth of the 225 richest people in the world.[lxix]

We may add that this social deficit could be covered by approximately 5% of world military expenditures.

The opposite pole of globalization is fragmentation – the exclusion of a majority of the world's population from the benefits of human development, generating a frustrated drive to defensive postures in violent and suicidal ideologies of nationalism, ethnicity and political-religious fundamentalism. Fault-lines are erected across the globe both vertically and horizontally by economic and military power relations on the one hand, and by gross inequalities between the rich and the poor on the other hand.

With ever more modernized conventional and nuclear weapons leaving the military laboratories, and human development in quandary, the world stands in awe at the opening of the new millennium, aspiring for salutary change.

Notes

Chapter 1: At the End of the Itinerary

i   See Marek Thee, "Note on the dividing lines between peace research and strategic studies" (the Lima paper), in Wilfried Graf, Ina Horn, Thomas H. Macho (Editors), Schriften zur Friedens- und Konfliktforschung, Band II, Verband der Wissenschaftlichen Gesellschaften Österreichs (VWGO), Wien 1989, pp. 298–305.

ii See Marek Thee, "The Post-Cold War European Landscape: Notes on the 'Velvet' Revolutions and Currents in Central Eastern Europe", Current Research on Peace and Violence, Vol. XIII, No. 2, 1990, pp. 57–64.

Chapter 5: The Indochinese Adventure

iii Notes of a Witness: Laos and the Second Indochinese War, New York: Random House, 1973. "The Dynamics of the Indochinese Conflict", Social Education, May 1970, pp. 519–542. "War and Peace in Indochina: US Asian and Pacific Policies", Journal of Peace Research, Vol. X, No. 1, 1973, pp. 51–70. "The Indochinese Wars: Great Power Involvement – Escalation and Disengagement", Journal of Peace Research, Vol. XIII, No. 2, 1976, pp. 117–129. "Red East in Conflict: The China-Indochina Wars", Journal of Peace Research, Vol. XVI, No. 2, 1979, pp. 93–100. "The China-Indochina Conflict: Notes on the Background and Conflict Resolution—the Case of Neutrality", Journal of Peace Research,

Vol. XVII, No. 3, 1980, pp. 223–233. "Towards a New Strategy for Conflict Resolution in Asia", Center for the Study of Armaments and Disarmament, California State University, Los Angeles: *Occasional Papers Series*, No. 9, 1982, 45 pp.

iv   Cf. Dwight Eisenhower, *Mandate for Change, 1953–1956.* London, 1963, p. 372.

v   *The Pentagon Papers*, The Defense Department History of United States Decision Making in Vietnam, The Senator Gravel Edition, 1971, p. 283.

vi   Anthony Eden, *Full Circle,* London: Cassel, 1960, p. 113.

vii   *Third Interim Report on the Activities of the International Commission for Supervision and Control in Laos, July 1–May 16, 1957,* New Delhi: Government of India Press, 1958, pp. 10–11.

viii   *Pentagon Papers,* Government Edition, Book 10, pp. 712–713.

ix   Text in N.S. Khrushchev, *Communism, Peace and Happiness for the Peoples,* Vol. I. (January–September 1961), Moscow: Foreign Languages Publishing House, 1963, pp. 37–45.

x   Arthur M. Schlesinger, Jr., *A Thousand Days: John F. Kennedy in the White House,* Greenwich, Conn.: Fawcett Publications, 1965, p. 282.

xi   *Pentagon Papers*, Senator Gravel Edition, Vol. II, p. 800.

xii   *Ibid*, pp. 637–642.

xiii   *Department of State Bulletin*, April 13, 1964.

Chapter 6: The Peace Research Chapter

xiv   *European Security and the Arms Race*, published in German under the title *Europäische Sicherheit und der Rüstungswettlauf*, in cooperation with Peace Research Institute Frankfurt, Campus Verlag, 1979, 296 pp. *Frontiers of Human Rights Education*, edited with Asbjørn Eide, in cooperation with UNESCO, Universitetsforlaget, 1983, 148 pp. *Arms and Disarmament: SIPRI Findings*, in cooperation with the Stockholm Peace Research Institute (SIPRI), Oxford University Press, 491 pp. *Preparation of Societies for Life in Peace*, in cooperation with the United Nations University Tokyo, Norwegian University Press, 1987, 261 pp. *Ethnic Conflict and Human Rights*, edited by Kumar Rupesinghe, in cooperation with the United Nations University Tokyo, Norwegian University Press, 164 pp. *Conversion of Military Production for Socially Useful Purposes*, edited with Lloyd J. Dumas, published by Pergamon Press under the title *Making Peace Possible: The Promise of Economic Conversion*, 1989, 317 pp.

xv   *Armaments and Disarmament in the Nuclear Age: A Handbook* (A SIPRI compendium to mark its 10th anniversary), Stockholm: Almqvist & Wiksell, and N.J.: Humanities Press Inc., 1976, 308 pp. (Translated and published in German, French, Japanese, Norwegian and Serbo-Croatian). *Problems of Contemporary Militarism*, edited with Asbjørn Eide (revised papers from conferences of the Pugwash Conferences on Science and World

Affairs, the World Council of Churches and IPRA), London: Croom Helm, 1979, 415 pp. *Armaments, Arms Control and Disarmament: A UNESCO Reader for Disarmament Education*, Paris: UNESCO, 1981/82, 446 pp.

Nuclear Disarmament in Europe, edited with Sverre Lodgaard (a SIPRI-Pugwash publication), London: Taylor & Francis, 1983, 271 pp.

xvi   *Notes of a Witness: Laos and the Second Indochinese War*, New York: Random House, 1973, 436 pp

Military Technology, Military Strategy and the Arms Race, in cooperation with the United Nations University, Tokyo, London: Croom Helm and New York: St. Martin's Press, 1986, 139 pp. *Whatever Happened to the Peace Dividend?* Nottingham: Bertrand Russel House, Spokesman, 1991, 113 pp.

xvii   Cf. Marek Thee, *Science and Technology: Between Civilian and Military Research and Development – Armaments and Development at Variance*, Geneva: UN Institute for Disarmament Research (UNIDIR), Research Paper No.7, November 1990, 21 pp.

xviii Cf. Marek Thee, "Disintegration of the Soviet Empire", *Current Politics and Economics of Russia*, Vol. 2, 1991, pp. 255–260.

xix   See Marek Thee, "The Scientist's Role in Society, An Outline of a Strategy", *Proceedings of the Twenty-Second Pugwash Conference on Science and World Affairs*, Oxford, England, September 7–12, 1972, pp. 551–555.

xx   *Ibid*, p. 555.

xxi   See full text in Marek Thee, "The Establishment of an International Disarmament Fund for Development: A Feasibility Study", *Bulletin of Peace Proposals*, Vol. 12, 1981, pp. 52–83.

xxii   United Nations, Study Series 5, *The Relationship Between Disarmament and Development*, New York, 1982, pp. 135–152.

xxiii Text in United Nations, *Establishment of an International Disarmament Fund for Development*, Geneva: UNIDIR, 1984, pp. 35–58.

xiv   *Ibid.*

xxv   UN Document A 39/229 of May 31, 1984. Also in UNIDIR, *The Establishment of an International Disarmament Fund for Development*, op.cit., pp. 3–33.

xxvi   *Report of the International Conference on the Relationship between Disarmament and Development*, Doc. A/CONF. 130/39, 22 September 1987.

xxvii UN Doc. A/CONF. 130/NGO and 131/NGO.

xxviii UN Doc. A/CONF 131/NGO.

xxix   See the summary paper: Marek Thee, "The Relationship Between Disarmament and Development: The Case for the Establishment of an International Disarmament Fund for Development", Oslo: *PRIO Working Paper 9/87*, December 1987; 18 pp; German version in *Dialoge*, Band 11, Heft 1–2, 1988, pp. 291–294.

xxx   Interview in *Development Forum*, Vol. XV. No. 6, July–August 1987.

xxxi   Text in *Bulletin of Peace Proposals*, Vol. 6, No. 3, pp. 262–280.

xxxii   Marek Thee, "Significance of Military R&D: The Impact of the Arms Race on Society", *Impact of Science on Society,* Vol. 31, No. 1, 1981, pp. 49–59.

xxxiii   Marek Thee, "The Race in Military Technology" in Joseph Rotblat (Ed.), *Scientists, the Arms Race and Disarmament,* London: Taylor & Francis, and Paris: UNESCO, 1982, pp. 49–56.

xxxiv   Marek Thee, "Military Research and Development: Its Impact on Society", in Kåre Berg and Knut Erik Tranøy (Eds.), *Research Ethics,* New York: Alan R. Liss, 1983, pp. 49–61.

xxxv   For the text of the Declaration see Marek Thee (Ed.) *Armaments, Arms Control and Disarmament: A UNESCO Reader for Disarmament Education,* op.cit, pp. 219–224.

xxxvi   United Nations, *Comprehensive Study on Nuclear Weapons,* New York, 1981, p.146, para 493.

xxxvii   See "Conclusions of the Second UN Special Session on Disarmament" 1983, *SIPRI Yearbook* , London and New York; Taylor & Francis, 1983, p. 556, para 59.

xxxviii UN Doc. A/RES/37/99J.

xxxix   On the course of drafting the UN study, see the paper by Ulrich Albrecht, who served as Consultant to the Group of Experts: "The Aborted United Nations Study on the Military Use of Research and Development", *Bulletin of Peace Proposals,* Vol. 19, No. 3–4, 1988, pp. 245–259.

xl   Text in *Proceedings of the Thirty-Sixth Pugwash Conference on Science and World Affairs,* London, pp. 357–360.

xli   *Ibid.*

xlii   Text in *PRIO Report,* No. 7, 1987.

Chapter 7: Aiming at a "Culture of Peace" Based on Human Rights

xliii   Marek Thee (Ed.), *PEACE! by the Nobel Peace Prize Laureates: An Anthology,* Paris: UNESCO Publishing, 1995, 570 pp.

xliv   Texts in *Human Rights: A Compilation of International Instruments,* Vol. I., First and Second Parts, New York and Geneva: United Nations, 1933.

xlv   See *European Social Charter* (revised 03.05.1996), Strasbourg: Council of Europe, 1996.

xlvi   See Marek Thee, "The Philosophical-Existential Issues of the Human Rights Project", in Bård-Anders Andreassen and Theresa Swinehart (Eds.), *Human Rights in Developing Countries Yearbook 1993,* Copenhagen Lund Oslo Åbo/Turku: Nordic Human Rights Publications, 1993, pp. 1–19. Marek Thee, UNESCO Peace and Conflict Series, *From a Culture of Violence to a Culture of Peace,* Paris: UNESCO Publications, 1996, pp. 229–250.

xlvii   Text in *Human Rights: A Compilation of International Instruments,* op.cit., pp. 544–549.

xlviii   Ibid, p. 543.

xlix   Cf. Manfred Nowak, *UN Covenant on Civil and Political Rights: CCPR Commentary,* Strasbourg: N.P. Engel, 1993, p. 851.

l   As of January 1998, the United States still kept a stockpile of 7256 nuclear warheads on bombers, Inter-continental Ballistic Missiles and Submarine-launched Ballistic Missiles. At the same time Russia had a stockpile of 6210 nuclear warheads on bombers, Inter-continental Ballistic Missiles and Submarine-launched Ballistic Missiles. See Robert S. Norris and William M. Arkin, "Tables on nuclear forces", Stockholm International Peace Research Institute, *SIPRI Yearbook 1988,* pp. 434–437.

li   Cf. Marek Thee, "The Doctrine of Nuclear Deterrence: Impact on Contemporary International Relations", in Yoshikazu Sakamoto (Ed.), *Strategic Doctrines and Their Alternatives*, New York, London, Montreux, Tokyo, Melbourne: Gordon and Breach Science Publishers, 1987, pp. 65–85.

lii   Cf. Ian Anthony, Pieter D. Wezeman and Siemon T. Wezeman, "The volume of transfers of major conventional weapons, 1988–97." Stockholm International Peace Research Institute, *SIPRI Yearbook 1998*, 1998, pp. 318–321.

liii   Cf. The Nobel Lecture by the Nobel Peace Prize Laureate, Prof. Joseph Rotblat, and the Nobel Lecture given by Prof. John P. Holdren, the Chair of the Executive Committee of the Pugwash Council, Oslo: The Nobel Committee, December 10, 1995.

liv   Cf. Marek Thee, "Demilitarizing International Relations and the Quest for a Human Rights Regime", *Proceedings of the Forty-Second Pugwash Conference on Science and World Affairs*, Vol. II, World Scientific: Singapore/New Jersey/London/Hong Kong, 1994, pp. 572–578.

Chapter 8: Epilogue: Plus Ça Change, Plus C'est La Même Chose

lv   Elisabeth Sköns, Agnès Courades Allebeck, Evamaria Loose-Weintraub and Reinhilde Weidacher, "Military Expenditure and Arms Production", *SIPRI Yearbook 1998,* Oxford University Press, p.185.

lvi   *Human Development Report 1998*, published for the United Nations Development Programme (UNDP), New York, Oxford: Oxford University Press, 1998, p. 37.

lvii   *Ibid.*

lviii Margareta Sollenberg and Peter Wallensteen, "Major armed conflicts", *SIPRI Yearbook 1988*, p. 17.

lix   *Human Development Report 1998,* op. cit., p. 35.

lx   See Eric Arnet, "Military Research and Development", *SIPRI Yearbook 1998,* op.cit., pp. 267–269.

lxi   *Ibid*, p. 271.

lxii   *Ibid*, p. 267.

lxiii Joseph F. Pilat and Paul C. White, "Technology and Strategy in a Changing World", *Washington Quarterly*, Vol. 13, No. 2, spring 1990, pp. 84–85.

lxiv   *Human Development Report 1998*, op.cit, Overview, p.1.

lxv   *Ibid*, p. 6.

lxvi   *Ibid*, p. 2.

lxvii   *Human Development Report 1998*, op.cit., Overview, p. 7.
lxviii *Human Development Report 1988*, op.cit, Chapter 1, p. 27.
lxix   *Ibid.*, p. 30.

Chapter 3
Marek Thee: His Published Work

Marta Bivand Erdal, Nils Petter Gleditsch, and Stein Tønnesson

Marek Thee was a prolific writer and made his mark in journalism as well as academic publications. What follows is hardly a complete bibliography, but we have been able to collect writings from four important periods of his life.

While in exile in Palestine, Marek served as an editor and publisher of *Biuletyn Wolnej Polski – Bulletin of Free Poland*. We have found two dozen articles in this journal from the period 1944–47, thanks to a bound volume left behind to his family. Most of his articles in *BWP* were written under various pseudonyms which are indicated in brackets after the bibliographic reference. His pseudonym Płom is short for Płommienny ('the fiery one'). The pseudonyms are listed in a 'thank you note' in the final issue of the journal in May 1947.

Following a period in the Polish foreign service, still based in Tel-Aviv, Marek returned to Poland in 1952 working first for the Polish foreign service and then for the Polish Institute of International Affairs. Because of his past affiliation with the foreign service, he again had to use a pseudonym and chose Marek Gdański, after his hometown. With help from the Polish National Library, we have been able to locate seven monographs and a number of journal articles from this period.

His Norwegian period started in 1968 and for the next twenty years he was attached to PRIO as a researcher at PRIO and as editor of the journal he founded, *Bulletin of Peace Proposals*. His very active scholarship during this period is reflected below in a large number of monographs, edited volumes, and articles. All under his own name!

Finally, after reaching the mandatory retirement age, he was invited to join the Norwegian Centre for Human Rights Institute at the University of Oslo and spent over ten productive years there until his death in 1999. His PRIO period and his Human Rights period are well covered in standard bibliographic reference sources, such as Web of Science, as well as in information supplied by the two institutes.

M. B. Erdal (✉) · N. P. Gleditsch · S. Tønnesson
Peace Research Institute Oslo (PRIO), Oslo, Norway

© The Author(s) 2023
M. Thee et al. (eds.), *Marek Thee: My Story*, SpringerBriefs on Pioneers in Science and Practice 32, https://doi.org/10.1007/978-3-031-16905-2_3

His diplomatic service in Indochina did not lend itself to diplomatic or journalistic writing, but is reflected in two of his books, most directly in his book about Laos from 1977.

Abbreviations used in the bibliography:
BPP – Bulletin of Peace Proposals
BWP – Biuletyn Wolnej Polski – Bulletin of Free Poland
JPR – Journal of Peace Research
SM – Sprawy Międzynarodowe (International Affairs)

Articles marked [Not signed] were probably written by Marek Thee, but the identification of the author is not completely certain.

The final section of this bibliography contains few items *about* rather than *by* Marek Thee.

3.1 Books

Thee, Marek (1956). *Bliski i Środkowy Wschód 1945–1955: Rywalizacja mocarstw zachodnich.* [The Near and Middle East 1945–1955: Rivalry between Western Powers. Warsaw: Książka i Wiedza. [Marek Gdański]

Thee, Marek (1957) (co-editor with R Borkowski, J Lobman, D Planer & A Szurek). *Konflikt izraelsko-arabski: Wybór dokumentów i materiałów* [The Israel-Arab Conflict: Selected Documents and Sources]. Zeszyty Dokumentacyjne (4/40). Warsaw: Polish Press Agency. [Marek Gdański]

Thee, Marek (1958). *Tło wypadków na Bliskim Wschodzie* [The Backdrop to Developments in the Near [Middle] East]. Warsaw: Wydawnictwo Drukarnia RSW 'Prasa'. [Marek Gdański]

Thee, Marek (1963) *Arabski Wschód. Historia, Gospodarka, Polityka* [The Arab East. History, Economy, Politics]. Warsaw: Ksiazka i Wiedza. [Marek Gdański]

Thee, Marek (1965). *Niespokojny Laos: Z dziejów kryzysu 1954–1964* [The Restless Laos: From the History of the Crisis 1954–1964]. Warsaw: Polish Institute for International Affairs. [Marek Gdański]

Thee, Marek (1973) *Notes of a Witness: Laos and the Second Indochinese War.* London: Random House.

Thee, Marek (ed.) (1976) *Armaments and Disarmament in the Nuclear Age: A Handbook.* SIPRI Books. Stockholm: Almqvist & Wiksell; Atlantic Highlands, NJ: Humanities Press.

Thee, Marek (ed.) (1977) *Rustninger og nedrustning i atomalderen* [Armaments and Disarmament in the Nuclear Age]. Oslo: Gyldendal.

Thee, Marek (ed.) (1979) *Europäische Sicherheit und der Rüstungswettlauf* [European Security and the Arms Race]. Frankfurt & New York: Campus.

Eide, Asbjørn & Marek Thee (eds.) (1980) *Problems of Contemporary Militarism.* London: Croom Helm.

Thee, Marek (ed.) (1981) Armaments, Arms Control and Disarmament. A UNESCO Reader for Disarmament Education. Paris: UNESCO.

Lodgaard, Sverre & Marek Thee (eds.) (1983) *Nuclear Disengagement in Europe.* London: Taylor & Francis.

Thee, Marek (1986) Military Technology, Military Strategy, and the Arms Race. London: Palgrave Macmillan.

Thee, Marek (ed.) (1986) *Arms and Disarmament: SIPRI Findings.* Oxford: Oxford University Press.

Dumas, Lloyd J & Marek Thee (eds.) (1989) *Making Peace Possible: The Promise of Economic Conversion*. London: Pergamon.
Thee, Marek (1991) *Whatever Happened to the Peace Dividend? The Post-Cold War Armaments Momentum*. Nottingham: Spokesman.
Thee, Marek (ed.) (1995) *PEACE! By the Nobel Peace Prize Laureates. An Anthology*. Paris: UNESCO.

3.2   Journal and Newspaper Articles

Thee, Marek (1944) Emigracja oderwana od kraju [Emigrants cut off from their country]. *BWP* (2): 3–4. MS]
Thee, Marek (1944) Francja upadek i powstanie [France: fall and rebirth]. *BWP* (13): 7. [Płom.]
Thee, Marek (1944) Na marginesie manifestu PKWN [Referring to the Manifesto by the Polish Committee of National Liberation]. *BWP* (11): 8. [Płom.]
Thee, Marek (1945) Decyzja zapadła na Wschodzie [A decision had been made in the East]. *BWP* II(24/43): 3. [Marek Tee]
*Thee, Marek (1945) Pobratymcy i sprzymierzeńcy [Friends and allies]. *BWP* II(30/49): 5. [Not signed]
*Thee, Marek (1945) Pobratymcy i sprzymierzeńcy [Friends and allies]. *BWP* II(39/58): 5. [Not signed]
*Thee, Marek (1945) Pobratymcy i sprzymierzeńcy [Friends and Allies]. II(40/59): 5. [Not signed]
*Thee, Marek (1945) Stosunki Polski z zagranicą [Foreign relations of Poland]. *BWP* II(45/64): 3. [Not signed]
*Thee, Marek (1945) Pobratymcy i sprzymierzeńcy [Friends and allies]. Przyjaźń z ZSRR [Friendship with USSR] *BWP* II(49/68): 5. [Not signed]
Thee, Marek (1945) Ze świata: Moskwa i Pearl Harbour [World: Moscow and Pearl Harbour]. *BWP* II(49/68): 5. [T.]
Thee, Marek (1945) Ze świata: Przy okrągłym stole [World: At the round table]. *BWP* II(50/69): 5. [T.]
Thee, Marek (1945) Ze świata: Persja na widowni [World: Persia on the scene]. *BWP* II(51/70): 5. [T.]
Thee, Marek (1946) Ze świata: Dobra wieść noworoczna [World: Good New Year's news]. *BWP* III(1/71): 11. [T.]
Thee, Marek (1946) Ze świata: Z lotu ptaka [World: From a bird's eye view]. *BWP* III(2/72): 11. [T.]
Thee, Marek (1946) OZN – Organizacja Pokoju [Camp of National Unity – An organization for peace]. *BWP* III(3/73): 5.
Thee, Marek (1946) Ze świata: Czujność w obronie pokoju [World: Vigilance for peace]. *BWP* III(7/77): 5. [T.]
Thee, Marek (1946) Ze świata: Walka z głodem [World: Fighting hunger]. *BWP* III(8/78): 5. [T.]
Thee, Marek (1946) Widma spod Verdun i dymy Majdanka [The ghosts of Verdun and smoke over Majdanek]. *BWP* III(9/79): 5.
Thee, Marek (1946) Reakcja polska pomaga Niemcom [Polish reactionaries help the Germans]. *BWP* III(30/100): 11.
Thee, Marek (1946) Długotrwały pokój [Long lasting peace]. *BWP* III(50/120): 5.
Thee, Marek (1947) Bagnety i dolary [Bayonets and dollars]. *BWP* IV(13/135): 1&6.
Thee, Marek (1947) Mówimy do was po raz ostatni [This is the last time we are addressing you]. *BWP* IV(19/141): 1. [Signed by The Editing Board, probably including Marek Thee]
Thee, Marek (1947) Pożegnanie z Biuletynem [A farewell to the Bulletin]. *BWP* IV(19/141): 4–5.
Thee, Marek (1947) Wracają [Going back]. *BWP* IV(16/138): 6.

Thee, Marek (1954) Za kulisami kryzysu marokańskiego [The backdrop of the Moroccan crisis]. *SM* 7(1/27): 74–79. [Marek Gdański]

Thee, Marek (1954) O wolność żeglugi na wodach Dalekiego Wschodu [For the freedom of shipping in the Far Eastern seas]. *SM* 7(3/29): 23–29. [Marek Gdański]

Thee, Marek (1956) Kryzys polityki bloków militarnych na Środkowym Wschodzie [The Political Crisis of the Military Blocs in the Middle East]. *SM* 9(4/48): 39–57. [Marek Gdański]

Thee, Marek (1956) Niektóre aspekty konfliktu sueskiego [Some aspects of the Suez conflict]. *SM* 9(10-11/55/56): 21–32. [Marek Gdański]

Thee, Marek (1957) Niektóre zagadnienia Środkowego Wschodu z perspektywy 1957 roku [Some topics of the Middle East in the perspective of 1957]. *SM* 10(12/69): 27–44. [Marek Gdański]

Thee, Marek (1958) Nowe momenty sytuacji na Bliskim Wschodzie [New Aspects of the Situation in the Near East]. *SM* 11(4/73): 46–71. [Marek Gdański]

Thee, Marek (1958) Bliski Wschód, lipiec–sierpień 1958 [The Near East, July-August 1958]. *SM* 11(9/78): 63–71. [Marek Gdański]

Thee, Marek (1958) III nadzwyczajna sesja specjalna Zgromadzenia Ogólnego ONZ [The Third Emergency Special Session of the UN]. *SM* 11(10-11/79-80): 125–133. [Marek Gdański]

Thee, Marek (1958) Irak – społeczne podłoże rewolucji republikańskiej [Iraq –the social basis of the republican revolution]. *SM* 11(12/81): 148–159. [Marek Gdański]

Thee, Marek (1959) Arabski Bliski Wschód u progu 1959 roku [Arab East at the verge of 1959]. *SM* 12(2/83): 20–43. [Marek Gdański]

Thee, Marek (1959) Układy wientiańskie [Vientiane agreements]. *SM* 12(10/91): 15–44. [Marek Gdański]

Thee, Marek (1960) Uwagi o kierunkach rozwojowych Arabskiego Wschodu [Comments on development directions of the Arab East]. *SM* 12(4/97): 112–120. [Marek Gdański]

Thee, Marek (1960) Cypr – niepodległość bez samookreślenia [Cyprus – independence without self-determination]. *SM* 13(10/103): 77–85. [Marek Gdański]

Thee, Marek (1960) Kryzys laotański na nowym etapie [The Laos crisis in a new phase], *SM* 13(11/104): 65–78. [Marek Gdański]

Thee, Marek (1961) Niebezpieczeństwo konfliktu w Laosie [The danger of a conflict in Laos], *SM* 14(2/107): 70–81. [Marek Gdański]

Thee, Marek (1961) Interwencja pod flagą ONZ – Likwidacja systemu kolonialnego – rewolucyjny proces dziejowy [Intervention under the UN flag – The liquidation of the colonial system – a revolutionary historical process]. *SM* 14(3/108): 10–32. [Marek Gdański]

Thee, Marek (1961) Wojna naftowa w Omanie [The Petroleum War in Oman], *SM* 14(4/109): 68–76. [Marek Gdański]

Thee, Marek (1963) Liga Arabska i problemy jedności arabskiej [The Arab League and the problems of Arab unity]. *SM* 16(2/131): 22–29. [Marek Gdański]

Thee, Marek (1964) Dyplomacja polska w międzynarodowych komisjach w Korei i Indochinach [Polish diplomacy in the International commissions in Korea and Indochina]. *SM* 17(7/148): 154–182. [Marek Gdański]

Thee, Marek (1964) Kryzys cypryjski – znaczenie międzynarodowe [The Cyprus crisis. Its international significance]. *SM* 17(10/151): 73–82. [Marek Gdański]

Thee, Marek (1964) Malajzja – ognisko napięcia w Azji [Malaysia – the hotbed of tension in Asia]. *SM* 17(11/152): 81–95. [Marek Gdański].

Thee, Marek (1965) Obalenie rządów wojskowych w Sudanie [The overthrow of the military rule in Sudan]. *SM* 18(2/155): 87–95. [Marek Gdański]

Thee, Marek (1965) Wojna w Indochinach – zagadnienia węzłowe [The war in Indochina – main issues]. *SM* 18(3/156): 76–106. [Marek Gdański]

Thee, Marek (1965) Rewolucja i ewolucja w Zjednoczonej Republice Arabskiej [Revolution and evolution in the United Arab Republic]. *SM* 18(6/159): 55–76. [Marek Gdański]

Thee, Marek (1965) Dylematy wojny amerykańskiej w Azji [The dilemmas of the American war]. SM 18(11/164): 21–45. [Marek Gdański]

Thee, Marek (1966) Jedność arabska w teorii i praktyce [Arab unity in theory and practice]. *SM* 19(5/170): 53–73. [Marek Gdański]

Thee, Marek (1966) Wokół polityki amerykańskiej w Wietnamie [On American policy in Vietnam]. *SM* 19(8/173): 102–118. [Marek Gdański]

Thee, Marek (1966) Sajgońskie wybory [Saigon elections]. *SM* 19(11/176): 82–93. [Marek Gdański]

Thee, Marek (1966) Souphanouvong – Souvanna Phouma. *SM* 19(12/177): 120–128. [Marek Gdański]

Thee, Marek (1967) Konflikt wietnamski – próba bilansu [The Vietnam conflict – an attempt at evaluation]. *SM* 20(1/178): 37–71. [Marek Gdański]

Thee, Marek (1967) Stany Zjednoczone i sprawa rokowań w konflikcie wietnamskim [The United States and the case of negotiations in the Vietnam conflict]. *SM* 20(5/182): 13–34. [Marek Gdański]ara>

Thee, Marek (1967) Konfrontacje wietnamskie [Vietnam confrontations]. *SM* 20(7-8/184-185): 92–117. [Marek Gdański]

Thee, Marek (1967) Tajne porozumienie w sprawie Indochin z 1954 roku [The secret agreement of 1954 on Indochina]. *SM* 20(11/188): 69–82. [Marek Gdański]

Thee, Marek (1967) Konflikt bliskowschodni – konfrontacja stanowisk (II) – wybór i opracowanie MG [The Middle East conflict – a confrontation of standpoints (II) – selection and presentation by MG]. *SM* 20(12/189): 97–117. [Marek Gdański]

Thee, Marek (1970) Prefatory note. *BPP* 1(1): 3–4. [The Editor]

Thee, Marek (1970) *Bulletin of Peace Proposals* – introduction. *BPP* 1(4): 291–292.

Thee, Marek (1970) Protracted Vietnam negotiations. *BPP* 1(1): 79–88.

Thee, Marek (1970) Dynamics of Indochina conflict. *Social Education* 34(5): 519.

Thee, Marek (chair); Eduardo P Archetti, Egil Fossum, Johan Galtung & Per Olav Reinton (1970) Development policies in Latin America – discussion on the proposals in Chapter 7. *BPP* 1(3): 277–285.

Eide, Asbjørn & Marek Thee (1972) Power politics and peace. Introduction. *BPP* 3(3): 195–198.

Thee, Marek (1972) The scientist's role in society. *BPP* 3(4): 367–370.

Thee, Marek (1972) Vietnam: The subtle art of negotiations. *BPP* 3(2): 163–171.

Thee, Marek (1972) Vietnamkrigen og forhandlingene [The Vietnam War and the negotiations]. *Internasjonal Politikk* 26(1): 71–84.

Thee, Marek (1972) US-Chinese rapprochement and Vietnam. *JPR* 9(1): 63–67.

Thee, Marek (1972) Tilnærmingen USA-Kina og forholdet til Vietnam [The rapprochment USA-China and the relationship to Vietnam]. *Samtiden* 81(2): 90–97.

Thee, Marek (1972) Krig eller fred i Vietnam? [War or peace in Vietnam] *Världspolitikens dagsfrågor* (10).

Thee, Marek (1973) Ending the war in Vietnam. *BPP* 4(1): 3–6.

Thee, Marek (1973) The international system after Vietnam: The three crucial spheres. *BPP* 4(4): 375–383.

Thee, Marek (1973) War and peace in Indochina – US Asian and Pacific policies. *JPR* (1–2): 51–70.

Thee, Marek (1973) Vietnamkrigens slutt [The end of the Vietnam War]. *Samtiden* 82(3): 129–135.

Thee, Marek (1974) Détente and security in the aftermath of the fourth Middle East war. *BPP* 5(1): 88–96.

Thee, Marek (1974) Disarmament through unilateral initiatives. *BPP* 5(4): 381–384.

Thee, Marek (1974) The nuclear arms race. *BPP* 5(4): 291–292.

Thee, Marek (1975) Atomvåpenkappløpet [The nuclear arms race]. *Samtiden* 84(1): 11–17.

Heradstveit, Daniel & Marek Thee (1976) Momentum for Arab-Israeli peace – introduction. *BPP* 7(4): 291–294.

Holst, Johan Jørgen; Erik Nord, Harald Munthe-Kaas, Anders C Sjaastad & Marek Thee (1976) Vietnam-krigen og dens perspektiver: Noen problemstillinger [The Vietnam War and its perspectives. Some approaches]. *Internasjonal Politikk* (1): 167–188.

Thee, Marek (1976) Arms control and disarmament. *BPP* 7(3): 278–377.

Thee, Marek (1976) Crisis in arms control – introduction. *BPP* 7(2): 99–102.

Thee, Marek (1976) Priorities in peace research. *BPP* 7(1): 69–74.

Thee, Marek (1976) Peace research and peace movements. *BPP* 7(1): 81–83.

Thee, Marek (1976) Militær forskning og dynamikken i rustningskappløpet [Military research and the dynamics of the arms race]. *Forskningsnytt* 21(3): 3–8.

Thee, Marek (1976) International arms control and disarmament agreements – promise, fact and vision. *International Social Science Journal* 28(2): 359–374.

Thee, Marek (1976) Indochina wars – great power involvement – escalation and disengagement. *Internationales Asienforum* 7(3–4): 204–231. Also as (1976) Krigene i Indokina: Stormaktsengasjement – opptrapping og avvikling. *Internasjonal Politikk* 34(1): 215–233.

Thee, Marek (1976) The nuclear arms race – trends, dynamics, control. *Instant Research on Peace and Violence* 6(1–2): 18–28. Also in: *Snage i putovi rata i mira*. Zagreb: Jugoslavenska Akademija Znanosti i Umjetnosti (557–572).

Thee, Marek (1976) Indochina wars – great power involvement – escalation and disengagement. *JPR* 13(2): 117–129.

Thee, Marek (1976) Weapons technology and disarmament negotiations. *Peace and the Sciences* (1): 77–82.

Lodgaard, Sverre & Marek Thee (1977) Arms race and nuclear proliferation – introduction. *BPP* 8(1): 3–6.

Lodgaard, Sverre & Marek Thee (1977) High military technology, security, and arms control. *BPP* 8(4): 291–295.

Thee, Marek (1977) Militarism and militarization in contemporary international relations. *BPP* 8(4): 296–309.

Thee, Marek (1977) Military variable of European détente. *BPP* 8(1): 47–48.

Thee, Marek (1977) Problems of European security and military détente. *BPP* 8(2): 150–152.

Thee, Marek (1977) Arms control – retreat from disarmament – record to date and search for alternatives. *JPR* 14(2): 95–114.

Thee, Marek (1977) Den militære verdensorden truer u-landenes selvstændighed [The military world order threatens the independence of the developing countries]. *Kontakt* 30(6): 7–10.

Thee, Marek (1978) Arms race, armaments dynamics, military research and development, and disarmament. *BPP* 9(2): 103–120.

Thee, Marek (1978) Failure of arms control, and strategies for disarmament. *BPP* 9(4): 375–377.

Thee, Marek (1978) Rustningskappløpet, rustningsdynamikken, militær forskning og utvikling, nedrustning [The arms race, the arms dynamics, military R&D, disarmament]. *Internasjonal Politikk* 36(2): 233–261.

Thee, Marek (1978) The dynamics of the arms race. Military R&D and disarmament. *International Social Science Journal* 30(4): 904–925.

Thee, Marek (1979) The China-Vietnam-Indochina conflict. The search for solutions. *Alternatives* 5(3): 351–367.

Thee, Marek (1979) European security and the arms race – findings of critical German peace research. *BPP* 10(1): 3–7.

Thee, Marek (1979) Arms control and security in Europe. Assumptions and essentials for alternative strategies. *Cooperation and Conflict* 14(4): 211–221.

Thee, Marek (1979) Some remarks on the SALT agreements – concerns of the peace research and disarmament community. *Current Research on Peace and Violence* 2(1): 12–19.

Thee, Marek (1979) Peace research in Oslo. *Development Dialogue* (1): 119–122.

Thee, Marek (1979) Security dilemma in Europe. *Peace and the Sciences* (1): 12–19.

Thee, Marek (1979) Red East in conflict – China/Indochina wars. *JPR* 16(2): 93–100. Also as: (1979) Det røde østen i konflikt. Krigen mellom Kina og Indokina. *Kontur* 3(3): 10–16.

Thee, Marek (1980) A world in tension – the drift from détente to confrontation. *BPP* 11(2): 105–107.

Thee, Marek (1980) Peace in the minds of men – thinking the unthinkable about war and peace. *BPP* 11(1): 3–8.

Thee, Marek (1980) Myten om freden i Europa [The myth of peace in Europe]. *Forsvar* 1(1): 12–14.

Thee, Marek (1980) Våbenkontroll i kronisk krise [Arms control in chronic crisis]. *Forsvar* 1(2): 18–21.

Thee, Marek (1980) Red East in conflict the China-Indochina wars. *Internationales Asienforum* 11(1–2): 5–16.

Thee, Marek (1980) The China-Indochina conflict – notes on the background and conflict resolution – the case of neutrality. *JPR* 17(3): 223–233.

Thee, Marek (1981) European security in the eighties – analytical and conceptual considerations. *BPP* 12(3): 225–238.

Thee, Marek (1981) The establishment of an International Disarmament Fund for Development – a feasibility study. *BPP* 12(1): 52–99.

Thee, Marek (1981) Waging nuclear war in Europe: Scenarios, consequences, alternative strategies. *BPP* 12(4): 365–421.

Thee, Marek (1981) Significance of military R&D – the impact of the arms race on society. *Impact of Science on Society* 31(1): 49–59.

Thee, Marek (1982) Halting the momentum of nuclear armaments – challenge and response. *BPP* 13(4): 283–289. Also as *PRIO Report* 3/82.

Thee, Marek (1982) Peace researchers and policy-makers. *BPP* 7(2): 161–162.

Thee, Marek (1982) Third-world armaments – structure and dynamics. *BPP* 13(2): 113–117.

Thee, Marek (1982) The Polish drama – its meaning and international impact. *JPR* 19(1): 1–10.

Thee, Marek (1983) Arms control and disarmament at a critical juncture on nuclear de-escalation in Europe. *BPP* 14(4): 299–303

Thee, Marek (1983) Scope and priorities in peace research. *BPP* 14(2): 203–208.

Thee, Marek (1983) Swords into ploughshares – the quest for peace and human development. *International Labour* Review 122(5): 535–548.

Thee, Marek (1983) Military research and development: Its impact on society. *Progress in Clinical and Biological Research* (128): 49–61.

Thee, Marek (1984) The state of the globe – rethinking problems of the nuclear arms race – peril and opportunity. *BPP* 15(4): 367.

Thee, Marek (1984) Problems of our nuclear predicament – arms control in crisis. *Current Research on Peace and Violence* 7(2–3): 81–89. Also as *PRIO Paper* 7/84.

Thee, Marek (1985) The arms race and the fate of Europe – the military-political nexus. *BPP* 16(4): 323–334. Also as PRIO paper 2/85.

Thee, Marek (1985) The arms race and the fate of Europe the military-political nexus *Current Research on Peace and Violence* 8(1): 13–23.

Thee, Marek (1986) Halting the nuclear arms race. Role of science and technology *BPP* 17(1): 41–46. Also as *PRIO Paper* 12/85.

Thee, Marek (1986) Military technology, the arms race and arms control. *BPP* 17(3–4): 535–538.

Thee, Marek (1987) Military technology, arms control and human development – reforging swords into plowshares. *BPP* 18(1): 1–11.

Thee, Marek (1988) Military use of research and development – the arms race and development. Letter from the editor. *BPP* 19(3–4): 243.

Thee, Marek (1988) Science and technology for war and peace – the quest for disarmament and development. *BPP* 19 (3–4): 261–292. Also in shortened form as: (1989) The Dynamics of the Technological Arms Race [with summary in German: Eigendynamik der Rüstungstechnologie]. *Interdependenz* (1). Bonn: Stiftung Entwicklung und Frieden. Also as: Recovering research and science. In: Ken Coates (ed.) *Perestroika: Global Challenge. Our Common Future*. Nottingham: Bertrand Russell House, 67–109. Reprinted in *ENDpapers* 17, 38–75.

Thee, Marek (1988) Antimatter technology for military purposes – excerpts from a dossier and assessments of physicists. *BPP* 19(3–4): 443–470.

Thee, Marek (1988) Zum Verhältnis von Abrüstung und Entwicklung. Argumente für die Einrichtung eines 'Internationales Abrüstungsfonds für Entwicklung' [To the relationship between disarmament and development. Arguments for the establishment of an 'International Disarmament Fund for Development']. *Dialog: Friedensbericht* 11(1): 288–294.

Thee, Marek (1988) The pursuit of a comprehensive nuclear test ban. *JPR* 25(1): 5–15. Also as *PRIO Report* 7/87.

Thee, Marek (1988) The Third Special Session of the UN General Assembly devoted to disarmament (SSOD-III): Between armaments and disarmament. *Transnational Perspectives* 14(3): 6–11. Also in: *ENDpapers* 18: 5–18.

Thee, Marek (1989) The quest for the demilitarization of international relations – openness versus secrecy in research and development. *Current Research on Peace and Violence* 12(4): 165–175. Also in: *PRIO Report* (5) and *Hiroshima Peace Science* (12).

Thee, Marek (1989) Military technology and the arms race. *Peace and the Sciences* (2): 63–77. Also as: Militärische Technologie und der Rüstungswettlauf: Das Streben nach Abrüstung und einem stabilen Frieden. *Wissenschaft und Frieden* (2): 43–58.

Thee, Marek (1989) Badania i zbrojenia a rozwój [Research and armaments and their influence on development]. *SM* 42(11): 37–54.

Thee, Marek (1989) The impact of military technology on disarmament and peace in Europe. *ENDpapers* 57: 43–58.

Thee, Marek (1989) The arms race: A new hype. *ENDpapers* (20): 7–19.

Thee, Marek (1989) Militärische Technologie und der Rüstungswettlauf [Military technology and the arms race]. *Wissenschaft und Frieden* (2): 43–58.

Thee, Marek (1990) Europe facing history – the imperative of comprehensive disarmament. *Current Research on Peace and Violence* 13(1): 1–5.

Thee, Marek (1990) The post-cold-war European landscape – notes on the velvet revolutions and currents in Central-Eastern Europe. *Current Research on Peace and Violence* 13(2): 57–64. Also as: (1990) Et europeisk landskap etter en kald krig. *Mennesker og Rettigheter* 8(4): 64–68.

Thee, Marek (1991) Die technologische Rüstungsspirale nach dem Golfkrieg – die Überwindung militärischer Technologie und ihre Konversion für menschliche Bedürfnisse [The technological armaments spiral after the Gulf War – overcoming military technology and converting it to human needs]. *AMI Antimilitarismus Information* (5): 20–24. Also (1992) as The post-Gulf War technological armaments spiral: Transcending military technology and conversion for human needs. *Peace Research* 24(1): 15–24.

Thee, Marek (1991) The post-Cold-War European landscape – the aftermath of the velvet revolutions in Central-Eastern Europe. *JPR* 28(3): 241–247.

Thee, Marek (1992) The post-Cold War European landscape. *Journal of East-West Studies* 21(1).

Thee, Marek (1992) Oppløsning av Sovjetunionen: Et grunnlag for demokrati [The dissolution of the Soviet Union: A basis for democracy]. *Mennesker og Rettigheter* 10(1): 27–32.

Thee, Marek (1993) Internasjonal demilitarisering og streben etter en menneskerettslig styreform [International demilitarization and the striving for human rights governance]. *Mennesker og Rettigheter* 11(1): 23–30.

Thee, Marek (1993) Retten til fred innebærer forbud mot atomvåpen [The right to peace implies a ban on nuclear weapons]. *Mennesker og Rettigheter* 11(4): 417–422.

Thee, Marek (1993) Stemmer fra Polen i en endringstid: meningsmålinger om demokrati og menneskerettigheter [Voices from Poland in a time of change: Public opinion polls on democracy and human rights]. *Mennesker og Rettigheter* 11(1): 106–109.

Thee, Marek (1994), Menneskerettigheter for en forandret verden [Human rights for a changed world]. *Mennesker og Rettigheter* 12(3): 230–239.

Thee, Marek (1997) En fredskultur bygget på menneskerettighetene [A culture of peace built on human rights]. *Mennesker og Rettigheter* 15(2): 132–144.

3.3 Articles in Edited Volumes

Thee, Marek (1954). Wstęp [Preface]. In: Alberto Jacoviello: *Spotkanie w Suezie* [A Meeting in Suez]. Warsaw: Książka i Wiedza, 3–4. [Marek Gdański]

Thee, Marek (1982) The race in military technology: Scientists, military R&D and the armaments momentum. In: Joseph Rotblat (ed.) *Scientists, Arms Control and Disarmament*. A UNESCO/Pugwash symposium London: Taylor & Francis (49–56).

Thee, Marek (1982) Militarism and human rights: Their interrelationship. In: Radakrishna Mahendra Agrawal (ed.) *Arms and Survival*. New Delhi: Satvahan (83–98).

Thee, Marek (1986) Military technology, the arms race and arms control. Ch 44 in: Marek Thee (ed.) *Arms and Disarmament: SIPRI Findings*. Oxford: Oxford University Press. (437–441).

Thee, Marek (1988) Between the arms race, arms control and disarmament. In: *Proceedings of the Thirty-Seventh Pugwash Conference on Science and World Affairs*, 501–504.

Thee, Marek (1988) Nuclear deterrence, minimum deterrence, deep cuts and the elimination of nuclear weapons. In: *Proceedings of the Thirty-Seventh Pugwash Conference on Science and World Affairs*, 505–510.

Thee, Marek (1988) The 'mad momentum' of armaments: Role of military technology in the arms race. In: Sven Hellman (ed.) *Disarmament – But How?* Stockholm: Swedish Professionals against Nuclear Arms (13–22).

Thee, Marek (1988) The impact of military technology on the arms race. In: F Stephen Larrabee (ed.) *Technology and Change in East-West Relations*. New York: Institute for East-West Security Studies (131–144).

Thee, Marek (1989) Note on the dividing lines between peace research and strategic studies. In: Wilfried Graf, Ida Horn & Thomas H Macho (eds) *Zum Wissenschaftsbegriff der Friedensforschung: Ergebnisse einer Umfrage*. Wien: Verband der Wissenschaftlichen Gesellschaften Österreichs (VWGO) (298–305).

Thee, Marek (1989) Military technology: A driving force behind the arms race and an impediment for arms control and disarmament. In: Hans Günter Brauch (ed.) *Military Technology. Armaments Dynamics and Disarmament*. London: Macmillan (39–64).

Eide, Asbjørn; Marek Thee et al. (1989) The Impact of the arms race on education, science and technology, and culture and communication' In: *UNESCO Yearbook on Peace and Conflict Studies*. Westport, CT & London: Greenwood & Paris: UNESCO (1–173). Also as *PRIO Report* 4/86.

Thee, Marek (1990) Science-based military technology as a driving force behind the arms race. In: Nils Petter Gleditsch & Olav Njølstad (eds) *Arms Races. Technological and Political Dynamics*. London: SAGE (105–120).

Thee, Marek (1992) The post-Cold War armaments momentum: Impact of military technology. In: Günther Bächler (ed.) *Perspektiven. Friedens- und Konfliktforschung in Zeiten des Umbruchs*. Zürich: Rüegger (217–233).

Thee, Marek (1992) The post-Cold War European landscape: Velvet revolutions and currents in Central and Eastern Europe in: Günther Bächler (ed.) *Perspektiven. Friedens- und Konfliktforschung in Zeiten des Umbruchs*. Zürich: Rüegger (157–170).

Thee, Marek (1992) The quest for openness versus secrecy in science and technology. In: Rilling et al. (eds) *Challenges: Science and Peace in a Rapidly Changing Environment*, Schriftenreihe Wissenschaft und Frieden, II(16), Bund Demokratischer Wissenschaftler.

Marek Thee (1994) Armaments and disarmaments in the post-Cold War period: The quest for a demilitarized and nuclear-free world. In: Volker Bonschier & Peter Lengyel (eds) *Conflicts and New Departures in World Society*. Piscataway, NJ: Transaction (61–69).

3.4 Book Reviews

Thee, Marek (1959) Review of Chatham House Study Group: British interests in the Mediterranean and Middle East. *SM* 12(1/82): 135–141. [Marek Gdański]

Thee, Marek (1959) Review of Caractacus: Revolution in Iraq. An essay in comparative public opinion. *SM* 12(11–12/92–93): 100–107. [Marek Gdański]

Thee, Marek (1960) Nauki «Zamkniętego koła» Sir Anthony Edena [Review of The teachings of the «Full Circle» by Sir Anthony Eden]. *SM* 13(6/99): 70–88. [Marek Gdański].

Thee, Marek (1980) Review of Peter Schier & Manola Schieroum (eds): Sihanouk of Cambodia – interviews and talks with Norodom Sihanouk. *Internationales Asienforum* 11(3–4): 386–387.

Thee, Marek (1985) Book Note on Ashton B Carter & David N Schwartz: Ballistic Missile Defense. *JPR* 22(2): 182.

Thee, Marek (1985) Book Note on Robert Ehrlich: Waging Nuclear Peace. *JPR* 22(2): 182.

Thee, Marek (1985) Book Note on Dietrich Fischer: Preventing War in the Nuclear Age. *JPR* 22(2): 182–183.

Thee, Marek (1985) Book Note on Daniel Frei: Assumptions and Perceptions in Disarmament. *JPR* 22(2): 183.

Thee, Marek (1985) Book Note on Bhupendra Jasani: Space Weapons: The Arms Control Dilemma. *JPR* 22(2): 183.

Thee, Marek (1985) Book Note on Brian Martin: Uprooting War. *JPR* 22(2): 183–184.

Thee, Marek (1985) Book Note on Steven E Miller: Strategy and Nuclear Deterrence. *JPR* 22(2): 184.

Thee, Marek (1985) Book Note on Burns H. Weston: Toward Nuclear Disarmament and Global Security: A Search for Alternatives. *JPR* 22(2): 185.

Thee, Marek (1985) Book Note on Andre Gunder Frank: The European Challenge: From Atlantic Alliance to Pan-European Entente for Peace and Jobs. *JPR* 22(3): 279–280.

Thee, Marek (1985) Book Note on Jozef Goldblat: Non-Proliferation: The Why and the Wherefore. *JPR* 22(3): 280.

Thee, Marek (1986) Book Note on Bill McSweeney (ed.): Ireland and the Threat of Nuclear War – The Question of Irish Neutrality. *JPR* 23(1): 89.

Thee, Marek (1986) Book Note on K Subrahmanyam: Nuclear Proliferation and International Security. *JPR* 23(1): 90.

Thee, Marek (1986) Book Note on Union of Concerned Scientists: Toward a New Security. Lessons of the 40 Years since Trinity. *JPR* 23(1): 91.

Thee, Marek (1986) Book Note on Gene Sharp: Making Europe Unconquerable – The Potential of Civilian-Based Deterrence and Defense. *JPR* 23(3): 301.

Thee, Marek (1986) Book Note on World Armaments and Disarmament: SIPRI Yearbook 1986. *JPR* 23(4): 400.

Thee, Marek (1987) Book Note on Rolf Berg & Adam-Daniel Rotfeld: Building Security in Europe: Confidence-Building Measures and the CSCE. *JPR* 24(1): 99.

Thee, Marek (1987) Book Note on Julian Lider: Correlation of Forces: An Analysis of Marxist-Leninist Concepts. *JPR* 24(1): 101.

Thee, Marek (1987) Book Note on Klaus Jürgen Gantzel & Jörg Meyer-Stauber: Die Kriege nach dem Zweiten Weltkrieg bis 1984. *JPR* 24(2): 205.

Thee, Marek (1991) Review of Common Responsibility in the 1990s: The Stockholm initiative on Global Security and Governance. *Mennesker og Rettigheter* 9(3): 308–310. [In Norwegian]

Thee, Marek (1993) Review of Michael Renner (1993): Critical Juncture: The Future of Peacekeeping. *Mennesker og Rettigheter* 11(3): 344–346. [In Norwegian]

Thee, Marek (1993) Review of John Dunn (ed.): Democracy: The unfinished journey 508 BC to AD 1993. *Mennesker og Rettigheter* 11(2): 262–264. [In Norwegian]

Thee, Marek (1994) Review of Geir Lundestad & Odd A Westad (eds) (1994): Beyond the Cold War: New Dimensions in International relations 90th Anniversary Nobel Jubilee Symposium. *Mennesker og Rettigheter* 12(1): 95–98. [in Norwegian]

Thee, Marek (1994) Review of Richard Pipes: Communism: The Vanished Specter. *Mennesker og Rettigheter* 12(3): 296–298. [in Norwegian]

Thee, Marek (1997) En verden i behov av lederskap. Review of Brian Urquhart & Erskine Childers: A World in Need of Leadership: Tomorrow's United Nations. A Fresh Appraisal. *Mennesker og Rettigheter* 15(1): 89–90.

3.5   Reports and Papers

Thee, Marek (1982) Towards a new conceptualization of neutrality: A strategy for conflict resolution in Asia. *Occasional Papers* (8 eller 9). Los Angeles, CA: Center for the Study of Armament and Disarmament, California State University.

Thee, Marek (1982) Halting the momentum of nuclear armaments: Challenge and response. *PRIO Report* (3).

Thee, Marek (1983) The establishment of nuclear-weapon-free zone in the Nordic countries. *PRIO Report* (1).

Thee, Marek (1983) Conversion of military-related industries to socially useful purposes. *PRIO Report* (8).

Thee, Marek (1983) Conceptual issues related to European security: Arms control and confidence-building measures. *PRIO Report* 9/83.

Thee, Marek (1983) Military research and development: An Asian perspective. *PRIO Report* (15).

Thee, Marek (1983) Modalities for the establishment of an international disarmament fund for development: Vision and political feasibility. *PRIO Report* (17).

Thee, Marek (1984) The state of the globe: Rethinking problems of the nuclear arms race. *PRIO Report* (4).

Thee, Marek (1984) Prevailing security doctrines and armament dynamics. *PRIO Paper* (9).

Thee, Marek (1984) Militarism and militarization: Their contemporary meaning. *PRIO Paper* (10).

Thee, Marek (1984) Threat perceptions in East-West relations: Strategies for change. *PRIO Paper* (12).

Thee, Marek (1985) The doctrine of nuclear deterrence. *PRIO Paper* (3).

Thee, Marek (1985) The dynamics of the arms race between the great powers. *PRIO Paper* (4).

Thee, Marek (1985) Role of military research and development. *PRIO Paper* (5).

Thee, Marek (1985) The Strategic Defense Initiative: A new turn in the arms race. *PRIO Paper* (8).

Thee, Marek (1985) Extension of the arms race into outer space and countervailing strategies. *PRIO Paper* (9).

Thee, Marek (1986) The race in military technology and arms control. *PRIO Paper* (4).

Thee, Marek (1986) Trust and mistrust in contemporary international relations. *PRIO Paper* (8).

Thee, Marek (1986) Peace research as a scholarly discipline. *PRIO Inform* (9).

Thee, Marek (1986) The strategic defence initiative and the arms race: Complementing nuclear exotic weapons. *PRIO Paper* (12).

Thee, Marek (1986) Constraining military technology: The civilizational imperative. *PRIO Inform* (12).

Thee, Marek (1986) The quest for an international fund for development. *PRIO Report* (13).

Thee, Marek (1986) Military technology, arms control and human development: Reforging swords into ploughshares. *PRIO Report* (15).

Thee, Marek (1986) War and peace in the contemporary world: Impact of modern military technology. *PRIO Report* (19).

Thee, Marek (1987) Impact of military technology on the arms race. *PRIO Working Paper* (1).

Thee, Marek (1987) Carrera armamentista y tecnologia y estrategia y estrategia militares. *PRIO Working Paper* (2).

Thee, Marek (1987) Nuclear deterrence, minimum deterrence, deep cuts, and the elimination of nuclear weapons. *PRIO Working Paper* (7).

Thee, Marek (1987) The relationship between disarmament and development – the case for the establishment of an international disarmament fund for development. *PRIO Working Paper* (9). Also as (1988): Zum Verhältnis von Abrüstung und Entwicklung. Argumente für die Einrichtung eines 'Internationales Abrüstungsfonds für Entwicklung. *Dialog Friedensbericht* 11(1–2): 281–294.

Thee, Marek (1989) Military technology – A driving force behind the arms race and an impediment to arms control and disarmament. 11th General Conference of the International Peace Research Association, University of Sussex, 13–16 April.

Thee, Marek (1990) Science and technology: Between civilian and military research and development: Armaments and development at variance. *UNIDIR Research Paper* (7).

Thee, Marek (1991) Disintegration of the Soviet empire – dangers and opportunities. *Occasional Papers* (47). Tampere: Tampere Peace Research Institute.

3.6 Other

Other writings by Marek Thee have been filed in PRIO's archive in the National Archives of Norway, in RA Privatarkiv PRIO 1955. 18 travel reports from the years 1982–86 authored or co-authored by Marek Thee are filed in Xj Travel reports. Marek's correspondence from 1975 to 89 is found in Dc. Other correspondence by Marek Thee is filed in Ad Bulletin of Peace Proposals.

3.7 About Marek Thee

Eckhoff, Torstein (1988) Internasjonal fredsforsker [International peace researcher; Marek Thee 70]. *Aftenposten*, 21 November: 12

Eide, Asbjørn (1999) Marek Thee [obituary, in Norwegian]. *Aftenposten* 29 April: 19.

Erdal, Marta Bivand (2019) The Lifelong Peace Advocate: A Portrait of Marek Thee (1918–1999). *PRIO Stories*, 19 June, https://blogs.prio.org/2019/06/the-lifelong-peace-advocate-a-portrait-of-marek-thee-1918-1999-by-marta-bivand-erdal/. Reprinted as Chapter 7 in Stein Tønnesson (ed.) (2022) *Lives in Peace Research. The Oslo Stories*. Singapore: Springer, https://link.springer.com/book/10.1007/978-981-16-4717-8.

Hirszowicz, Łukasz(1964) Review of Marek Gdański: Arabski wschód. Historia, gospodarka, polityka. *SM* 17(7/148): 183–187.

Lobman, Jerzy (1966) Review of Marek Gdański: Niespokojny Laos. *SM* 18(1/166): 208–210.

Stański, Z (1957) Review of Marek Gdański: Bliski i Środkowy Wschód. *SM* 10(4/61): 135–141.

Thee, Halina (2020) Radio Blog in Norwegian on her family's life in and expulsion from Poland. *Sommer i P2*, NRK, https://radio.nrk.no/serie/sommer-ip2/sesong/202006/MKRH03000820.

About the Co-editors

Nils Petter Gleditsch (born 1942) is a Research Professor at the (http://en.wikipedia.org/wiki/Peace_Research_Institute_Oslo) (PRIO). Following studies in Oslo and Ann Arbor, Michigan, Gleditsch graduated from the University of Oslo as mag.art. in sociology. Since 1964, he has been affiliated with PRIO), first as a student, later as researcher, serving as Director in 1972 and 1977–78. Gleditsch was editor of Journal of Peace Research 1983–2010. He is professor emeritus of political science at the Norwegian University of Science and Technology (NTNU) in Trondheim. He served as President for the (http://en.wikipedia.org/wiki/International_Studies_Association) (ISA) 2008–09. In 2009, Nils Petter Gleditsch was given the *Award for Outstanding Research* by the (http://en.wikipedia.org/wiki/Research_Council_of_Norway). He is a member of the Royal Norwegian Society of Sciences and Letters (DKNVS) and the (http://en.wikipedia.org/wiki/Norwegian_Academy_of_Science_and_Letters).

Address: PRIO, P O Box 9229, Grønland, 0134 Oslo, Norway

Email: nilspg@prio.org

Website: www.prio.org/staff/npg

M. Thee et al. (eds.), *Marek Thee: My Story*, SpringerBriefs on Pioneers in Science and Practice 32, https://doi.org/10.1007/978-3-031-16905-2

Stein Tønnesson (b. 1953) is Research Professor at the Peace Research Institute Oslo (PRIO). He is a historian with a Dr Phil from the University of Oslo in 1992 and has been affiliated with PRIO for three periods since 1981, most recently as Director of PRIO (2001–09) and Research Professor since 2009. He has also been a Research Professor at the Nordic Institute for Asia Studies in Copenhagen (1992–98), an adjunct professor of human development studies at the University of Oslo (1998–2001), and Head of the East Asian Peace program at Uppsala University (2011–16). He is a member of the Norwegian Academy of Science and Letters (DNVA).

Address: PRIO, P O Box 9229, Grønland, 0134 Oslo, Norway

Email: stein@prio.org

Website: www.cliostein.com

Marta Bivand Erdal (b. 1979) is a Research Professor in Migration Studies at PRIO, with a Ph.D. from the University of Oslo (2012). She has worked at PRIO since 2007. As a Human Geographer she is interested in the impacts of migration and transnationalism in emigration and immigration contexts, mainly in South Asia and Europe. She now serves as Co-Director of the PRIO Migration Centre. She was a member of the Young Academy of Norway, 2017–21, and in 2019 she received the Fridtjof Nansen Award for younger scholars in science and the humanities.

Address: PRIO, P O Box 9229, Grønland, 0134 Oslo, Norway

Email: marta@prio.org

Website: martabivanderdal.org

About the Book

Marek Thee was a Jewish Polish journalist, scholar, and activist. This book tells his life from narrowly escaping death in the Holocaust to exile in Palestine, where he became attached to the Polish consular service. On his return to Poland in 1952, he worked for the Foreign Ministry and later for the Polish Institute for International Affairs. He served as Head of the Polish delegation to the International Control Commission in Indochina from the late 1950s. In 1968 he lost his job and his Polish citizenship in a nationalistic and antisemitic campaign. He was able to move to Norway where he worked for twenty years at the Peace Research Institute Oslo (PRIO), editing an international quarterly journal, Bulletin of Peace Proposals and doing research on the arms race. In retirement, he continued his research and writing at the Norwegian Human Rights Institute. The book vividly relates the drama of his life in Poland, Palestine, Indochina, and Norway.

- Marek Thee's life mirrors key events in international relations in the twentieth century.
- His outspokenness and independence led him into conflict with the Nazi regime as well as Stalinist Poland.
- His academic work dealt with crucial issues like war and peace, development, and human rights
- Marek Thee is a stellar example of a fighter with a typewriter

The book is edited by Nils Petter Gleditsch, Marek Thee's colleague at PRIO for twenty years. Gleditsch has previously published three books in the Springer 'Pioneer' series (in 2015, 2917, and 2020), all of them open access and frequently downloaded.

The first co-editor is his colleague Stein Tønnesson, a historian and a recognized academic expert on Indochina, who was also a long-time colleague of Marek Thee's. Tønnesson also served as Director of PRIO (2001–09).

© The Editor(s) (if applicable) and The Author(s) 2023   109
M. Thee et al. (eds.), *Marek Thee: My Story*, SpringerBriefs on Pioneers in Science and Practice 32, https://doi.org/10.1007/978-3-031-16905-2

The second co-editor is Marta Bivand Erdal, a research professor at PRIO and a specialist in migration. While she never met Marek Thee in person, she was commissioned to write an essay on Marek Thee for an oral history project at PRIO, published in *PRIO Blogs* and as Chapter 7 in Stein Tønnesson (ed.) (2022) *Lives in Peace Research. The Oslo Stories.* Singapore: Springer, https://link.springer.com/book/10.1007/978-981-16-4717-8.

CVs for the three co-editors can be found on their homepages at PRIO.

Printed by Printforce, the Netherlands